Help for the Children

Help for Dyslexic Children

T. R. Miles, MA, Ph.D, FBPs.S

and

Elaine Miles, MA, Dip.Ed.

London and New York

First published 1983 by Methuen & Co. Ltd
Reprinted by Routledge 1989, 1991, 1994
11 New Fetter Lane, London EC4P 4EE

Simultaneously published in the USA and Canada
by Routledge
29 West 35th Street, New York, NY 10001

Much of this material originally appeared in
T.R. Miles *On Helping the Dyslexic Child*
and T.R. Miles and Elaine Miles
More Help for Dyslexic Children.

This edition © 1970, 1975, 1983 T.R. Miles and Elaine Miles

Photoset by Rowland Phototypesetting Ltd.
Bury St. Edmunds, Suffolk
Printed in Great Britain by Richard Clay Ltd.,
Bungay, Suffolk

British Library Cataloguing in Publication Data

Miles, T.R.

Help for dyslexic children.
   1. Dyslexia   2. Reading—Remedial teaching
   I. Title   II. Miles, Elaine
   371.91′4   LB1050.5

Library of Congress Cataloging in Publication Data

Miles, T.R. (Thomas Richard).
   Help for dyslexic children.

   'Based on the authors' two earlier volumes, On helping the dyslexic child ·
and More help for dyslexic children'—p. iv.
   Bibliography: p.
   Includes index.
   1. Dyslexic children—Education. I. Miles, Elaine.
II. Miles, T.R. (Thomas Richard). On helping the dyslexic child.
III. Miles, T.R. (Thomas Richard). More help for dyslexic children.
IV. Title.
LC4708.M54   1983   371.91′4   83-921

ISBN 0-415-04570-3

Contents

Preface

Our two earlier books, *On Helping the Dyslexic Child* and *More Help for Dyslexic Children*, are here presented as a single volume. During the process of reorganization we have taken the opportunity to up-date the material in a number of ways.

Knowledge of how best to help dyslexic children has in fact advanced considerably in the last few years, and since the original books were first published we have been able to draw not only on our own increased experience but on the results of discussion with co-workers in many different parts of the world. In addition the conclusions of the two earlier books were of necessity somewhat tentative: we were able to report on what we ourselves had found helpful but there was at the time no documented evidence that the procedures which we used would necessarily be effective if used by other people in other contexts. Such evidence is now available in the form of a research paper.[1] After outlining methods which are in relevant respects similar to those described in this book, the authors of this paper report how they collected evidence from three different centres where these procedures were used (one of which was our own Dyslexia Unit). Only 5 out of 107 children failed to make significant progress; the average gains in reading ages and spelling ages, with an average teaching period of about 20 months per pupil, were 1.40 months per month and 1.62 months per month respectively. The evidence does not show that other methods would not have worked, but it certainly shows that there were many children who made quite striking improvements; and, as the authors point out, there are good

1. See B. Hornsby and T. R. Miles, 'The effects of a dyslexia-centred teaching programme', *Brit. J. Educ. Psychol.*, 50, 1980, 236–42.

reasons for believing that the results were not due to what is called the 'Hawthorne effect' (that is, improved performance not because of the method used but solely because of the feeling that someone is trying to help). In addition, it has even been possible to suggest reasons why these particular methods are effective: basically it is because the dyslexic child has special difficulty in handling symbolic material; and if we think of each person's brain as able to acquire a set of standards – a kind of internal lexicon or dictionary – against which any new stimulus can be compared, there is good evidence that the lexicon of a dyslexic person is in some way faulty, since he[2] usually needs a longer time than a non-dyslexic person to 'take in' arrays of words, letters, or numbers and produce the correct response. There is therefore a striking coherence between some of the recent theoretical thinking on the subject of dyslexia and the fact that certain teaching procedures have been proved to be effective.[3]

It is important, however, that those who teach dyslexic children should not be so tied to a single method that they become inflexible in their approach. Indeed, what is offered in this book can only with reservations be called a 'single' method at all. If one had to describe it in a single sentence, one would perhaps say that the teacher should progressively show the pupil the ways in which sounds and combinations of sounds are represented by letters and combinations of letters in the English spelling system. In this book we have indicated the sort of way in which this can be done, while still leaving a considerable amount to the discretion of the teacher.[4]

With regard to acknowledgements, we have learned so much from so many people that we feel it would be invidious to mention individual names. We should like to pay tribute, however, to the many fellow-members of the British Dyslexia Association with whom we have exchanged ideas and also to a large number of members of the Orton Dyslexia Society in the USA. Coming nearer home we

2. Throughout this book we shall use the word 'he' rather than the more cumbersome 'he or she', though what is said applies, of course, to girls no less than to boys.
3. For further discussion of this point see T. R. Miles and N. C. Ellis, 'A lexical encoding deficiency II', in G.Th. Pavlidis and T. R. Miles (eds), *Dyslexia Research and Its Applications to Education*, Chichester and New York, John Wiley & Sons.
4. American teachers should be alerted to the need for adjustments on the few occasions in this book when British and American spellings differ. The English place names in Appendix II can of course be changed provided words of equally simple phonic pattern are substituted.

owe a particular debt to our colleagues at the Dyslexia Unit, University College of North Wales, Bangor, both research workers and teachers, for the many ways in which they have helped us. We should also like to thank the officials of the Gwynedd Local Education Authority for giving us the opportunity to teach dyslexic children in state schools. Finally we are grateful to Mrs Llio Ellis Williams for her unfailing skill in converting illegible manuscript into neat typescript.

T.R.M.

E.M.

Bangor, 1982

Chapter 1

Introduction

The aim of this book is a practical one, viz. that of making suggestions we hope will be of value to parents, teachers and others in providing dyslexic children with the help that they need. Theoretical issues have therefore been kept as far as possible in the background.

Since, however, there has been some degree of controversy (or, perhaps one should rather say misunderstanding and argument at cross purposes) about the existence and nature of dyslexia it may perhaps be of help if we indicate briefly the conclusions to which we have been led as a result of our experiences in the last twenty years.

During this time we have met many children who were clearly not just 'slow' or 'stupid' and who had had all the normal opportunities in school but who nevertheless showed quite striking difficulties in reading and spelling. One of the things which regularly emerged during assessments was that it was the same *pattern* of difficulties which kept recurring – a pattern which we shall describe in more detail in Chapter 2 – and the accumulated evidence left us in no doubt that these regularities were something more than mere coincidence.

It was also clear that when the difficulties occurred they could not be attributed to poor teaching, to cussedness on the part of the child, or to inappropriate pressures on the part of the parents. The children whom we saw had received many different kinds of teaching; many of them, so far from being cussed, were desperately anxious to learn, and while we met many concerned and anxious parents it would have been arrogant for us to say that they were *over*-anxious or *over*-protective; and we found nothing to suggest that these parental attitudes were the main source of the children's difficulties. Both from our own experience and from an examination of the literature it was plain that the difficulties often occurred in more than one member of the same family, and there was ample evidence that they occurred more often in boys than in girls, the ratio being about 3 ½ or 4 to 1.

These facts pointed inescapably to the conclusion that the difficulties were constitutional in origin; that is to say, there was something in the child's physical make-up which prevented the normal acquisition of certain skills with words and other symbols. This view was further confirmed when we examined the literature on so-called 'aphasic' adults – those with disorders of thought and speech as a result of acquired brain injury: their mistakes, though varied, were in some ways very like the mistakes which we ourselves were meeting, for example a failure to put words and other symbols in the correct order in space and time. There was no good reason for supposing that more than a few of the children whom we met had undergone actual brain *damage*, but there was every reason to suspect some kind of failure of development or some kind of stunted growth which resulted in mistakes analogous to those made by brain-injured adults. The precise details of what causes dyslexia are not yet fully known, and indeed it is possible that the same pattern of difficulties may not always have the same cause; but that some kind of constitutional limitation is involved seems to us to be established beyond any reasonable doubt.

To describe a person as dyslexic, therefore, is to say that he displays a characteristic pattern of difficulties, with the implication that these difficulties are of constitutional origin.[1]

There has in fact been some rather fatuous argument as to the value of the term 'dyslexia', much of which, we suspect, is due to misunderstanding. If, as a parent, you are given conflicting advice on this point, we suggest that you rely on those who genuinely seem to you to understand your child's difficulties. If you are a teacher we suggest that you try to find out more about these difficulties so as to ensure that the advice which you give is helpful and constructive. In our view the actual *word* 'dyslexia' is unimportant, since a word

---

1. When we use the word 'dyslexia' in this book we are, of course, referring to *developmental* dyslexia, that is, a weakness in initially learning particular language skills, as opposed to *acquired* dyslexia where skills already learned have been affected by brain damage.

of approximately equivalent meaning would do as well, such as 'specific learning disability'. What is important is the orientation – the particular view of the child's difficulties – which use of the word implies.

It is sometimes said that parents and child are discouraged or demoralized when they are told that the child is dyslexic. In our experience this is almost never the case, at least if the word is properly explained to them. On the contrary they are often very much relieved. The reason seems to be that when one gives parents information about typical cases of dyslexia this makes sense of what would otherwise have seemed extremely bewildering. We have often met parents who could tell that *something* was wrong, without knowing what; and if one can make clear that the child is suffering from a recognized disability about which certain fairly probable predictions can be made, this makes it much easier for them to give the appropriate kind of support. Similarly, if teachers can be told, not, 'Here is yet another backward reader,' but, rather, 'Here is a child *with a disability which requires special understanding*,' it will be possible for them to help the child in a constructive way.

To sum up, there seem to us to be three main advantages in using the word 'dyslexia' (or some equivalent expression): it classifies, it explains, and it invites to action.

As far as classification is concerned, use of the word forces educationalists to distinguish those who are failing because they have a constitutional limitation from those who are failing because of lack of intelligence or opportunity; and it is disastrous in practice if this distinction is not noticed. As far as explanation is concerned, the fact that the difficulties are constitutional in origin calls for an adjustment of standards, since if a person is handicapped this is quite different from being 'not very good' at a particular task. Finally, if a person is dyslexic, it is important that *something should be done* for him; it is inexcusable in the light of present-day knowledge of teaching methods that any child in our educational system of average ability or above should be allowed to fail at reading and spelling simply because his problem has not been properly recognized.

Chapter 2

What to look for

If you suspect that your child is dyslexic, we suggest in the first place that you consult with his class teacher and, where appropriate, his head teacher. It may often be helpful if the child receives a complete assessment from an educational psychologist, and in that case we suggest that you ask for full details of the findings.

We strongly advise that you assume goodwill in the first place; and indeed there are reasonable grounds for optimism since understanding of dyslexia is far more widespread now than it was a few years ago. If, however, you have any reason to be dissatisfied with the treatment that your child is receiving or if his teachers do not appear to have understood the position when you yourself feel that there is something wrong, then even if you are reluctant to appear to be 'making a fuss' we strongly suggest that you do not let the matter rest there. You yourself have lived with your child over many years, and if you are dissatisfied our experience suggests that you may well be right. For suggestions as to where to go for help see p. 113.

Moreover, even if there is some doubt about the diagnosis – as there may well be, for instance, in the case of a six- or seven-year-old – we have found that it is far wiser to assume that the child *is* dyslexic than to assume that he is not. Little is lost if one pays special attention to his reading and spelling at this age, and if the diagnosis is mistaken then his progress will be correspondingly more rapid. In contrast, if he is dyslexic but through high intelligence or other means has managed to 'cover up' so that his handicap is not fully apparent, the lack of early help is likely to be disastrous for him. It is also disastrous if well-meaning teachers attempt to reassure the parents of a dyslexic child by saying, 'Don't worry; he is a late developer and it will come'. We have seen far too many families who have been given this advice and after taking no action for several years have found that the hoped-for progress has *not* come. One needs to be very sure indeed, in our view, before deciding that a child is *not* dyslexic.

Perhaps the most important question that you should ask yourself is whether the child's performance leaves you with a sense of incongruity. This can arise in particular if he is weak at reading and spelling (or, in some cases weak at spelling only) when in other respects he does not behave like a dullard at all. For example, he may be good orally and show high-level reasoning ability; he may have considerable electrical and mechanical skills; he may be outstandingly gifted at art or woodwork – yet when he tries to put his ideas down on paper he may fare far worse than many less gifted children.

It is of course important to use common sense and not jump to the conclusion that a child is dyslexic on too slender evidence. He may be failing at reading and spelling simply because he is not very bright, or perhaps because he has been absent from school. He may be suffering from the effects of some serious shock, for example a death or divorce in the family. In all these cases, however, one would expect a more generalized kind of failure, involving all school subjects, not the specific *pattern* of difficulties which one finds in dyslexia.

In practice the diagnosis is made as a result of the accumulation of a number of different signs, any one of which would be of no special significance on its own. The mistakes and confusions which we shall be describing in this chapter are mistakes and confusions which all of us make from time to time; it is simply that the dyslexic person makes more of them and makes them more frequently.

One of the most common signs is that the child shows persistent uncertainty as to which way round to place letters and figures, for example by misreading *b* for *d* or *p* for *q* or by making the corresponding mistakes in writing them. Thus a boy whom one of us taught misread *boys* as 'dogs', while among spelling errors we have met 'tolq' for *tulip* and 'catqil' for *caterpillar*. Sometimes the letters of a word are in the wrong order, for example 'brian' for *brain*. You should not, of course, take mistakes of this kind too seriously when they are made by five- and six-year-olds; they are very common in the early stages of learning to read and write, and the great majority of children grow out of them by the age of seven or eight at the latest. In a dyslexic child, however, they sometimes persist well beyond this age. Also it can sometimes happen that although the mark which eventually appears on the page is the correct way round, say *b* and not *d*, earlier crossings out show that there was a large amount of uncertainty in the first place.

There is a complication in the case of spelling errors in that it is not always clear whether a particular error is a mistake over direction as such or whether the child is simply unsure – as a result of general confusion – what letter to put next. Thus if one finds 'whte' for *with* in a school exercise book one cannot tell whether the child is making a 'back-to-front' mistake over the *t-h-* or whether (as seems to us more likely) this is not a directional or 'reversal' error as such but is the result of guesswork and a vague feeling that the word should begin with *wh*.

Often the spelling is very strange in appearance. Illustrations are given on pp. 8–9.

Both the examples on p. 8 were copied from school exercise books, and as neither of us was present at the time we do not know what either child was trying to say. On p. 9, however, are two further examples where, despite the oddity, it is possible to tell what was intended with some degree of confidence.

Although not all dyslexic children spell as strangely as this, these extreme examples are useful in that they exhibit in a particularly striking way the kinds of mistake which dyslexic children are likely to make. You will notice that an attempt is often made to use the sounds of the letters as a guide to spelling but that in the end-product many things seem to have gone wrong. For example, when *ask* in Sample 3 is spelled 'rsg' this suggests that the boy was confused between the name of the letter *r* and its sound; when he writes 'feouf' for *five* he is confusing *f* and *v*, presumably because their sound is similar. 'Sepedns' and 'sopsts' for *substance* in Sample 4 represent a similar confusion, this time between *b* and *p*. 'On' in Sample 4 would have been a plausible attempt at *own* but shows lack of familiarity with the *-ow* pattern which occurs in words such as *low*, *mow*, etc. 'Soled' for *solid* shows lack of awareness that *-ed* is a past tense ending and therefore inappropriate here. The inconsistent spellings of *substance* and *liquid* illustrate the difficulty, shown by many

WEAHER

When nolot conome a lot of winper it is
had or differur do make a Globben with
my Soch wilon is Kownom heed

Dain

I am writen to un a bot the nonl-set.
ther at prol at the whos clop at ambnar. Homo
amon you get en from your frot you praocties
the nori of ynes.

Yuro argust-

one day feorf chulir went
to rog theymother wech will.
we b going for nw hotday

Sample 3   One day five children went to ask their mother, Where shall we be going for our holiday?

Wen a soled sepdns lwzsis it
on fram, and is advanead in a liwecaa,
we ser the sopnts has drosand in
the lwecaed.

Sample 4   When a solid substances loses its own form, and is absorbed in a liquid, we say the substance has dissolved in the liquid.

dyslexic persons, in remembering what they have written a moment earlier. Since these children were known to be intelligent in other ways their difficulty with spelling seems the more incongruous.

This kind of spelling is sometimes referred to as 'bizarre' spelling; and there is good reason for thinking that bizarre spelling and directional confusion regularly go together.

Here are some additional signs of dyslexia, though they do not occur in every case. Sometimes the handwriting is curiously awkward, as in the case of Sample 1. Sometimes the child is reported as being clumsy in his movements, and in some cases there is evidence of speech difficulties. A very large percentage are unable to learn arithmetical tables and many have difficulty with addition and subtraction, some of them finding it necessary to use their fingers or marks on paper and then carry out the operation one unit at a time. In many cases there is difficulty in reciting the months of the year and, among younger children, the days of the week. Some are late in learning to tell the time, and many have difficulty in remembering strings of numbers, for example telephone numbers. Some are unable to repeat longer words orally without getting the syllables in the wrong order, for example the words *preliminary* and *statistical*.

In brief, then, a dyslexic child is one who has (or has had) unusual difficulty with both reading and spelling, his performance being discrepant with what might be expected from his intellectual level. Often he muddles *b* and *d* at an age when other children no longer do so. His spelling is frequently *bizarre* in the sense described above, and at least some of the signs mentioned in the last paragraph will almost certainly be present in a way which cannot just be coincidence.

A concluding note. The use of standardized tests

If there is any doubt as to a child's general ability or level of educational attainment, arrangements can be made for him to take standardized tests. In this context we are thinking in particular of intelligence tests and tests of reading and spelling. When a test has been standardized, this means that it has been given to a large number of children – probably thousands – and that figures are available which show what is the average or expected performance for children of a given age. On the basis of the results you can then tell how far a particular child is above or below the average.

In the case of dyslexic children, however, various cautions are necessary. Thus, in trying to reach an assessment of their intellectual level, one needs to remember that there are items in traditional intelligence tests which cannot be correctly answered unless the child can read the instructions; dyslexic children may therefore fail the item not because it is too difficult intellectually, but simply because of their reading difficulty. Also some test items place special demands on immediate memory for symbolic material, and in these cases, if a dyslexic child fails, this may be simply an indication of his special disability, not an indication of lack of intelligence. A simple adding up of correct answers is therefore likely to give a false picture. Consequently, if you have been told the IQ figure for a dyslexic child, it would be wise, we believe, to treat it with caution; and if you are familiar with intelligence tests in general, you may find it helpful to obtain precise information as to which test items he passed and failed. If he has been successful in some very difficult items, this should certainly be taken seriously, even if he has failed some of the easier ones; and in general it seems to us that you would be right to regard a high score as an important piece of evidence, even if in the case of a low score you decide to reserve judgement.

In addition to intelligence tests one can also give the child tests of attainment at reading and spelling. If the child is a long way behind the average for his age, the problem of remedial education becomes all the more urgent. It is of course important to examine the kinds of mistake which the child makes as well as considering his actual score.

If you want further evidence as to whether the child is dyslexic you may like to consider using the Bangor Dyslexia Test.[2] We are not necessarily suggesting that you should give the test to your own child; you may prefer to ask someone else to do so. Either way, however, the results can be used as a supplement to the information which you already have about the child, and the results may in some cases 'tip the scale' in determining you to ask for further help. If you give this test we particularly advise that you read the instruction manual carefully.

The main advantage of using standardized tests is that one is then

2. Obtainable from Learning Development Aids, Duke St, Wisbech, Cambs.

in a position to compare a child's attainment at reading and spelling with his intellectual level. It does not, of course, follow that all children who show a discrepancy between intelligence and attainment are dyslexic, but where such a discrepancy is accompanied by some of the other signs which we have described (or which occur when the child is given the Bangor Dyslexia Test) the likelihood that he is dyslexic becomes very much greater. This means that he is not simply 'a poor reader' but that his difficulties are of constitutional origin and that they will not be properly understood unless this point is recognized.

Chapter 3

Help at home and at school

In Chapter 4 and subsequent chapters we shall be suggesting ways of helping dyslexic children with reading, writing, spelling, and arithmetic. Before we do so, however, we should like to make suggestions as to other kinds of help which they are likely to need both at home and in school. This chapter is addressed to both parents and teachers.

The central point to appreciate is that the dyslexic child is carrying a handicap. Once you realize this you will come to see his problems – and some of the irritating things which he does – in a new light.

If a child has an obvious disability, for example if he is lame or paralysed, both he and the adults at least know what to expect. Even in the case of a child who is slow at learning and is put in a special class, the problem is manageable and clear. For a dyslexic child, however, unless his dyslexia is recognized, there must always be the nagging uncertainty in his own mind, 'Am I stupid? Am I mad? Why am I different from the others?' Vague, unformulated fears are perhaps even more unpleasant than a clearly recognized disability; and in this connection we should like to quote what seems to us to be a telling sentence from *The Pirate*, by Sir Walter Scott: 'The most cruel wounds are those that make no outward show.' In view of what they have been up against, it has always seemed remarkable to us that so many dyslexic children are as resilient and happy as they are.

Parents and teachers, therefore, need continually to make clear to a dyslexic child that they are willing to try to understand his difficulties. The amount of effort required from a dyslexic child to produce a given result (for example a piece of written work or the answer to a problem in arithmetic) is much greater than that which would be required from a non-dyslexic child of similar age and ability. We should like to illustrate this point by means of two examples.

In the first place, if you look at the following pattern (Fig. 1)

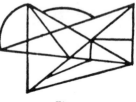

Fig. 1

for a brief instant, you may well have considerable difficulty in reproducing it correctly. Unless you know Hebrew the same will be true in the case of Fig. 2.

Fig. 2

If, however, you look at Fig. 3, you will be able to reproduce it at once,

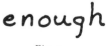

Fig. 3

just as those familiar with Hebrew are easily able to reproduce Fig. 2, which is the Hebrew word for 'wilderness'. The point of showing you Figs. 1 and 2 and then showing you Fig. 3 for comparison is to exhibit the difference between those marks on paper which are meaningful and those which are not. For the dyslexic child – at least in the early stages – there is no such contrast; all marks on paper beyond a certain degree of complexity are equally meaningless. Now in your own case, if you had sufficient incentive – and I am sure this incentive would need to be very great! – you might be willing to learn the full intricacies of Fig. 1 by heart, and perhaps a few more figures of similar complexity. But imagine yourself being required to learn a thousand such shapes! In point of fact, since you are lucky enough not to be dyslexic, those shapes which we call *words* are meaningful to you, and you can correctly reproduce (or 'spell') not a thousand but perhaps forty thousand or more of them. For a dyslexic child, however, the shapes which you can easily identify as words are recognized only after considerable effort, and even more effort is needed if he is to reproduce them in spelling. Requiring him to learn words by heart, therefore, is to impose an impossible strain on his memory, and our experience is that correct recall of the spelling lasts at most for only a few days. We have noticed also that a dyslexic child, in the early stages of learning to read and spell, is not as troubled by crossings out as is the non-dyslexic person. For example, if he wrote *preach* as *peash*, his corrected effort might be *preach*. To the rest of us this is more uncomfortable than *preach*, though to him the second is likely to be about as bewildering as the first.

Secondly we should like to quote some material found in the exercise book of a dyslexic child when he was asked to do some calculation.[3] The question which he was asked was 'How many twos are there in one hundred?' What he wrote in his exercise book was:

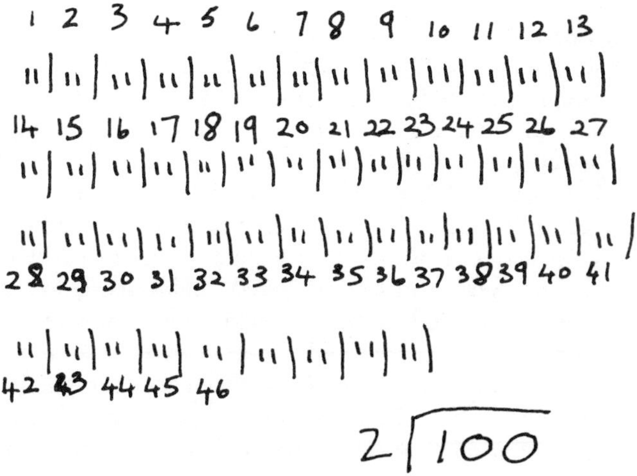

Fig. 4

---

3. We owe this example to our colleague, Mr J. M. Griffiths.

This example shows not only the need for 'concrete representation' of particular numbers (compare Chapter 7) but – what is particularly relevant in the present context – the enormous amount of time and effort which is needed by a dyslexic child in some circumstances if he is to reach the correct answer. Only when this boy had written the number 46 above one of his groups of two tally-marks was he confident enough to count ahead and give the answer as 50.

We are sometimes amazed at the extent to which dyslexic children are willing to make such efforts. Praise for effort on the part of adults is therefore extremely desirable; and it is, of course, particularly disappointing for a child if he has put heart and soul into, say, a piece of free writing and his book is then returned to him with adverse comments such as 'Your spelling is appalling; take more trouble.' A sympathetic teacher will grade such written work on content rather than on spelling; and if you feel that *some* reference to the weak spelling has to be made for fear of seeming to condone low standards there is no reason why you should not say, for example, 'I understand Miss X is helping you with spelling so I did not write in any corrections.' This conveys that you understand his difficulties but avoids giving him the impression that you think spelling unimportant.

Because the dyslexic child is carrying a handicap you will need to adjust your standards in deciding when to praise and when to find fault or express concern. Praise rather than blame is of course very desirable; and if you can genuinely say, 'Your spelling has improved' this may well give him a much-needed fillip. False reassurance seems to us to be harmful, however, since if in fact he is making little progress with his spelling it is likely that he will know this only too well. In any case one owes it to any child to make clear what one expects of him. A home or school where a child is free to do just as he pleases seems to us undesirable as well as unworkable in practice; one is in effect saying to the child, 'I don't *care* whether or not you saw the legs off the piano; I don't *care* whether or not you hurt the cat.' It seems to us perfectly possible, without reverting to old-fashioned authoritarian methods, to make clear that one *does* care. We are not suggesting that one should 'blame' children in any harsh sense, but one owes it to them to comment on how well or badly they are doing.

It follows, of course, that if a dyslexic child fails at the spelling of an irregular word or if he correctly applies rules which you have given him but the word in question happens to be spelled differently, then any form of adverse criticism is out of place. If, however, he fails to do what *by his standards* is perfectly possible for him, admonition of the form, 'You can do this if you try', seems perfectly appropriate. Even so, perhaps one should be careful, since for several years others will have been saying to him, 'You can do it if you try', in situations where he has tried very hard and yet still been unsuccessful.

The more you can appreciate what he can do and cannot do, the more he will trust you as someone sympathetic to his difficulties. In our experience different children react to their dyslexia in different ways. Some show extra dogged determination; some may become discouraged or withdrawn; some may – quite understandably – indulge in anti-social behaviour (though expressions of sympathy, such as 'No wonder you felt like this,' can often be of help in such cases provided one does not seem to be 'getting at' the child), while a few may 'act the clown' or, at least outwardly, pretend not to care.

Once it is appreciated, however, by the child himself, by his parents, and by his teachers that there is a specific disability, tensions arising from such behaviour are likely to disappear. The child will recognize that there is no need to feel ashamed or act aggressively towards other people. It is important, incidentally, if a headmaster or headmistress knows a child to be dyslexic, that this information should be passed on to all the child's teachers. Otherwise the sensitive efforts of several adults in building up confidence may be undone by the insensitive action of a single teacher who reverts to the earlier charges of laziness, carelessness or lack of effort. It is sometimes helpful, too, if the dyslexic child and his parents can learn to laugh at some of his mistakes. 'You silly idiot! You've gone and muddled up left and right again!' is basically a sympathetic remark since it shows understanding of the difficulties, and there may be many occasions when friendly laughter can help to remove tension.

There may, of course, be extra problems if an older child is dyslexic while his younger brother or sister is not; it is not surprising if the dyslexic child feels a certain reluctance to accept help! Our experience suggests that frank discussion is the most appropriate answer. As usual, it is misunderstanding which seems to create the problems, and if everyone knows what kinds of thing a dyslexic child finds difficult a major cause of unhappiness is removed.

It is worth bearing in mind that there are many different ways in which a young dyslexic child is affected by his handicap. If he is a poor reader, this will not only affect his school work and cripple his progress in almost all school subjects; it also limits his experience outside school. In countless ways he is not being stimulated. The result is that he is continually missing the opportunity to learn what is going on in the world around him. He fails to notice, for instance, the range of bus services in his home area, and he has no reason to wonder why mail vans have *Royal* written on them. Separately these points may seem trivial, but cumulatively the loss of experience is considerable.

Similarly, it is a matter of familiar experience that dyslexic children are often weak at arranging things in the correct order, such as the months of the year, and many of them show uncertainty over times and dates. Even those who in other respects are obviously intelligent may be unable to say what month it is or give the month and year of their birth. Several are reported to have shown confusion over *time* words, e.g. by using 'yesterday' when they meant 'tomorrow'; and one older boy, according to his parents, did not always seem to know the correct day of the week or time of day; thus he might announce that he was 'off to the shops', either forgetting that it was a Sunday or not noticing that it was 7.30 in the evening when all shops would be shut.

Not all dyslexic children make such mistakes, but it seems important that parents and teachers should be alerted to this kind of possibility. One cannot help wondering if an insecure sense of time may sometimes make it impossible for some of them to 'look forward' to things, for example to Christmas day or to their birthday. Difficulty with arithmetic is perhaps part of the same handicap. To work out for oneself that it is eighteen days to Christmas one has not only to know that it is now 7 December and that Christmas day is 25 December; one has also to be able to subtract seven from twenty-five. It may therefore help a dyslexic child if he is shown how a calendar works or if he is told that a particular event will take place soon or in a few weeks. One cannot take for granted that he has learned this kind of thing for himself.

There may also be problems over getting things organized – getting to school in time, remembering to include the right things in the satchel and so on. For example, if a child is uncertain over time the fact that an appointment has been fixed for 2 p.m. may not have been properly understood; and if he turns up at 2.30 he could well be rebuked for his selfishness and lack of consideration for others. If Wednesday is the day for football his failure to bring his football boots may have arisen because of some uncertainty over days of the week. Encouragement to find ways of overcoming his distinctive difficulties is likely to be more effective than simply blaming him for being selfish or careless.

We have met on occasion children who did not like their class-mates to know about their difficulties. Clearly one would not in these circumstances put pressure on the child to publicize his dyslexia. It is certainly a strain, however, to have to keep 'covering up'; and ideally one looks for a climate of opinion where dyslexia is understood and accepted and where there is no need for the dyslexic person to feel 'different' in any unpleasant sense.

We have also met teachers who have expressed reluctance to make allowances for a dyslexic child on the grounds that they must treat all the class alike. Such an approach seems to us somewhat inflexible, and it is again reasonable to hope for a climate of opinion in schools where *any* child with special needs can have these needs taken into account. Provided the general principle of 'special allowance for special needs' is accepted there is nothing inequitable in taking a dyslexic child's special needs into account.

We have also been concerned to note the *unnecessary* strain to which parents of dyslexic children have sometimes been exposed. The tradition, alas!, seems to die hard in some educational circles that if a child has problems with reading or is misbehaving this is invariably due to disturbed relationships within the family. We have found that all too often parents of dyslexic children have been told by 'experts' – or at least allowed to believe – that their own anxiety was the main cause of the child's difficulties. (Such 'experts' often seem reluctant to consider even the possibility that the child is suffering from a constitutional disability; and it seems hard to understand why such alleged anxieties should result in failure at specific tasks, such as reading, spelling, saying numbers backwards, etc., and should not extend, for example, to oral work or to art.)

Three examples from our experience must suffice. In one case the father of a bright dyslexic boy of ten was asked by an educational organizer, 'What have you *done* to the boy to make him like this?' In another case the mother of an exceptionally bright dyslexic boy of thirteen had parted from her husband; not surprisingly she was made to feel that the boy's difficulties were the direct result of the disruption of the home. Thirdly, there was the case of a woman who had adopted three boys but who was herself unmarried. One of these boys, though bright, was in fact found at age nineteen to be severely dyslexic, with a special weakness at tasks involving short-term memory. Time and time again this woman had been led to believe that absence of a father was the main causal factor (this, despite the fact that this absence had *failed* to produce dyslexia in two of her three sons!). If parents are subjected to such treatment, whether implicitly or explicitly, our advice is that they should not take it seriously.

They may also be accused of being 'over-protective'. Here again it seems to us desirable that they should use their own judgement as to what the child needs rather than be put off by what others think he ought to need. We have regularly found that a dyslexic child may be two years, or even more, behindhand when it comes to taking examinations such as CSE and O level. We also have reason to suppose that in some cases dyslexia can hold back general emotional maturity. Thus it may well be – at least in these cases – that a dyslexic child is in need of a certain amount of extra 'mothering'; and we very much hope that fear of seeming to be what is unkindly called in some circles an 'anxious mum' will not prevent mothers from giving a dyslexic child the attention which they can see is necessary.

It is sometimes implied that the notion of dyslexia is an invention by over-ambitious middle-class parents who cannot accept the fact that their child is none too bright and wish to make some further excuse for his failure in school. Our experience does not bear this out. We have in fact met few cases where the parents believed their child to be dyslexic and were mistaken, though occasionally we have met cases where the child's other needs (e.g. for psychiatric help) were more pressing. We have, however, met plenty of cases where the child was in fact dyslexic but where the parents made clear that, if the child was found simply to be rather slow, this would not distress them unduly. Sneers that dyslexia is a middle-class invention are unkind and unjustified.

Another piece of educational folk-lore which seems to need challenging is the view that parents should never attempt to teach their own children. On several occasions we have in fact invited mothers (and on one occasion a father) to sit in for a week while the child received daily lessons from our own teachers, and we have then encouraged them to take over the teaching. We do not wish to minimize the amount of patience and skill which this arrangement calls for, nor to press parents into such an arrangement against their better judgement. Certainly both the parent and the child need to be prepared for a hard slog; but we think it important that parents should not be discouraged from the attempt simply because 'experts' have led them to doubt their own competence.

In this connection we are reminded of the situation where a husband teaches his wife to drive a car; this works in some cases and not in others! It is perhaps less easy for a parent than for an outsider to strike the right balance between pressing the child too hard and not pressing him hard enough, and if the child feels that his parents do not understand his difficulties this is likely to be more distressing to him than if there is lack of understanding from someone outside the family. These objections, however, are not insuperable, and, at least in the case of some families, teaching by the parents may well be the correct answer.

We are sometimes asked what are the long-term prospects for a dyslexic child. It is difficult to answer with any high degree of assurance. We are in no doubt that it is possible for those with dyslexia to achieve considerable success in many different fields, since we have met people who have done so. Passing the necessary examinations may take longer, and quite a number of adults with residual dyslexic signs have reported to us that they are still poor spellers and (in some cases) slow readers. It seems likely, therefore, that the difficulties do not disappear completely, but our experience suggests that they can be largely compensated for and are unlikely to cause permanent unhappiness. We suggest that a dyslexic child should be allowed to go at his own pace and that parents should be open-minded in their expectations for his future.

Once parents have understood the difficulties experienced by their dyslexic child, the everyday provision of help and support is in large measure a matter of common sense.

Chapter 4

Help for the seven-year-old

If your child is still having difficulty with reading by the time he reaches the age of seven you may well have come to suspect that something is not quite right. If this is so, there are a number of things which you can do in quite an informal way so as to help him.

It is likely that he is still unsure of some of the sounds made by letters of the alphabet. To teach him these you should obtain sets of letters made of wood or plastic and let him see and feel them. There are two main ways of checking his knowledge. The first is to present him with a letter and get him to tell you its sound; the second is to make the sound yourself and ask him to pick up or point to the correct letter from a choice of two or more letters laid out on the table. It is worth making a special check on the less frequently used letters such as *k*, *v*, *w*, *x*, *y*, and *j*.

When you introduce the vowels, give him only the *short* vowel sounds, viz.

a as in *apple*
e as in *egg*
i as in *ink*
o as in *orange*
u as in *umbrella*

In the case of consonants you should try as far as possible to 'clip' the sound at the end. In the case of the letter *p*, for example, you should bring the lips together so as to make the *p*-sound but avoid calling it 'per'. *Y* should be sounded as in *yellow* and its two vowel sounds (as in *by* and *happy*) should not be taught until later. In the case of the consonants *c* and *g* you should teach only the hard sound in the first place, as in *cat* and *goat*, not the soft sound as in *city* and *giant*.

Teaching of letter sounds can be carried out without its seeming like a lesson. If your child is interested in trains, for instance, you could ask him to take the engine to the shed marked '*j*'. Another child may enjoy it if you point to things in the room such as the *w*all, a *k*ettle, or some *j*eans, and ask him to show you the letter which makes the sound at the beginning, or you could ask him to think of things which start with that sound. I-spy is a good game to adapt for this purpose provided you use the sound rather than the name of the letter. If in fact he knows the names as well, so much the better, but there is no need for them to be specially taught nor at this stage is it necessary for him to learn the alphabet by heart.

Some teachers encourage the pupil to trace the shape of letters 'in the air' or in sand; and this will provide yet another way of making the different letters familiar. It is also helpful to ask him to say the letter aloud before pointing to it or writing it. The purpose of these procedures is to enable him to learn the links between what he sees (the visual appearance of the letter), what he hears (its sound), what he feels in his mouth when he says it, and what he feels 'in the air' or in sand when he traces it. Many of the books on dyslexia speak of 'multisensory' learning, and this is the kind of thing which they have in mind.

At an early stage it may be helpful if you can explain to him that consonants and vowels do a different job. Although in general it is undesirable to make a dyslexic child learn any large number of technical terms, the words 'consonant' and 'vowel' are important enough to be exceptions. If it helps, you should explain that consonants are letters which are formed with the lips, teeth, and tongue, whereas these are not used in the case of vowels. You may like to show him some typical three-letter words such as *mat* and *hen* which are made up of consonants on the outside and a vowel – like the soft centre in a piece of chocolate – in the middle.

If he finds the short vowel sounds difficult, it may be easier for him to start with a whole word, for example *cat*, *hen*, *pig*, *dog*, or *cup*,[1]

1. These are in fact the words which we suggest for inclusion at the top of page 1 of the dictionary (see p. 65). In the present chapter, however, we are concerned with the kind of informal training which can be given before the formal work on the dictionary is started.

and work out what the sound in the middle is in each case. Once he knows the letter sounds (or even a limited number of these, provided there are some vowels) he will himself be able to build words with his wood or plastic letters. He will also be able to say what letter is needed to complete a word (for example if a picture of a hat were accompanied by the letters *h-t*) and to read simple three-letter words from cards. It is helpful if at an early stage he can learn to read the word 'in one' rather than by sounding out each letter separately.

These ideas can be incorporated into various games. For example you could invent a version of rummy or Happy Families in which the player collects pictures of objects beginning with the same sound or a board game in which the player picks up a card when he reaches a certain square and loses a turn if he cannot say the sound correctly. For some of these games blank playing cards may be useful (for a source of supply see p. 108).

There are a number of readers (reading books) which will be suitable for him at this level. We particularly recommend *Primary Phonics*, Set 1, and *More Primary Phonics*, Set 1, and *One Way with Words* (for details see p. 107). These are fun to read, and, since they are short, he will be able to complete the story in one or two sittings. This gives particular encouragement to children who have been going very slowly through an unsuitable school book, taking a long time, and are then given the boring task of having to read it again in the hope that they will do better. Provided you choose readers which use only the sounds which the child has already learned, you can insist that he reads every word correctly. Other suggestions for readers, work books, and materials are given on pp. 107–9.

When he is reading aloud we suggest that you resist the temptation to rush in and help him on all occasions. If the book is at the right level for him he will know the relevant letter sounds, and in that case if he goes wrong all that you need to do is to stop him and get him to have another look at the letters, so that he can think again about their sounds. If he succeeds you should praise him liberally; he will be able to see for himself that he was not 'just guessing' and that the praise was deserved.

It is, of course, very important that you yourself should read aloud to him. For this purpose you can, of course, choose books which are appropriate for his intellectual level rather than books which he himself can read; and you may like to encourage him to *listen* carefully to sounds. (In this connection we recommend *The Iron Man*, by Ted Hughes, because of the clanking metallic sounds which occur in the story.) If he can get used to the idea that stories are fun he will be more inclined to put in some extra effort when he experiences difficulty in reading to himself.

Writing may also be a problem for him. You can help in the first place by making sure that he holds his pen or pencil between the thumb and first two fingers in such a way that he can manipulate it easily in all directions. (The three-sided nylon grips mentioned on p. 108 may be a help if his movements seem awkward.) Felt pens are useful, and he may enjoy making patterns such as those set out in Fig. 5, which were done by a severely dyslexic boy aged 15.

When you give him practice at writing make sure that he starts each letter in the correct place and consistently uses the same movements for the same letter. You may find it helpful to group the letters according to their starting point. Thus the following letters should be started on the right:

a, c, d, g, o, q, s,

and the following on the left:

r, m, n, p, i, j, v, w, x, y, z, u

while the following should start at the top of the 'stick':

l, h, b, k, t, f

e is the odd one out and starts in the middle.

You can also use writing practice as a way of helping him to distinguish between *b* and *d*. If these two letters are started correctly the risk of confusion is considerably lessened.

The suggestions made in this chapter are put forward as activities which you and your child can carry out for pleasure with a minimum of formality. If he is dyslexic he may have a tendency to 'shy away' from letters and other symbols, and it will be a great help if you can show him that they are things to be enjoyed. If all has gone well he will now be ready to start some more formal work on 'building a dictionary'.

Fig. 5 Writing patterns made by Christopher W., aged fifteen.

Chapter 5

Building a dictionary

Introduction

We are assuming that the child now knows the sounds made by the different letters. It is wise, however, before you start the programme, to check that this is so, using the procedure indicated in the previous chapter, i.e. by presenting him with letters and asking him to make the correct sound and by giving him sounds and asking him to choose or write the correct letter.

When he knows the letters he should write them inside the cover of the dictionary which you are now about to build. If you turn to the Sample Dictionary (Appendix I, p. 64) you will see how this can be done. You will notice that the consonants and vowels are laid out separately so as to emphasize their different functions.

When you get to the digraphs (*sh*, *th*, *ch*, and *wh*) these, too, can be added, and similarly with the blends[1] (*cr*, etc.) and the letter combinations which occur at the end of words (*-ll*, etc.). *ph* should not be introduced until later.

When you pass to the exercises we suggest that you read each sentence aloud and that the pupil repeats it back to you before he writes anything. Any part of the sentence can, of course, be repeated to him if necessary; and the longer sentences occurring in later exercises can be taken in two halves.

In the early exercises very few words of more than one syllable have been included; but when such words are introduced for the first time we have sometimes divided the syllables by a prime sign (′); this

1. For an explanation of these terms see pp. 31 and 32.

is to remind you to repeat the word part by part and thus ensure that he does not move on to the second syllable until he has completed the first.

No exercise should be given until he has been introduced to the requisite sounds. The exercises have in fact been numbered in such a way that they indicate what pages of the dictionary are being tested. For example, Exercises 4A and 4B assume that he has been introduced to all the sounds as far as Page 4 of the dictionary. There are two reasons why it is important not to ask him to read or spell words for which he has not yet been given the sound. In the first place, by including the word in a dictation you are implying that you expect him to get it right; and since a dyslexic child can seldom spell words unless he has specifically learned them or been shown their pattern you are being unfair to him. Secondly, the whole point of the method is to make clear to him that if he pays attention to the sounds he can work out what letters to put. (He may sometimes come across 'funny' words where this procedure does not work; but we have not introduced these until later in the programme so that in the early stages he can build up confidence by correctly spelling regular words.)

This does not mean avoiding all new words. If, for example, he has learned the short *a* sound and has been given the words *hat* and *bag* he can also be expected to spell *rag*. Plenty of new words like this are introduced in the exercises. They can, of course, be added to the dictionary when convenient, and join the family to which they belong. It is, however, a crucial principle in teaching dyslexic children that one should show them what to do in advance. Rather than letting them go wrong and then correcting their mistakes you should create the conditions where they do not go wrong in the first place.

The approach which we adopt here has been designed so as to reduce to a minimum the amount of rote learning needed. A number of books recommend the learning of spelling rules by heart, but in our experience a dyslexic child finds such learning so difficult that he is unlikely to benefit and may well become discouraged. Instead we have tried to help him to understand the way in which the English spelling system works and in particular to show him what 'jobs' are done by the different letters. This puts him in a position where he can use his reasoning skills and does not need to rely on his memory.

The first page

By dividing Page 1 of the dictionary into five columns one is sorting words out according to the vowel sound in the middle. If the pupil is asked to point to the correct column for a particular word this forces him to listen very carefully to the central vowel sound before writing the word down.

At the start it may be wise not to give him more than two columns to choose from. Since we recommend starting with the short *a* and short *i* columns (see below) this means that you could tell him that *cat* has an *ă* sound (short *a*) and *pig* an *ĭ* sound (short *i*)[2] and that all words with an *ă* sound should go in the first column and all words with an *ĭ* sound in the third column. As soon as he has understood what is involved, you should ask him to tell you the correct columns for other words, such as *hit*, *hat*, *sad*, *him*, *lid*, etc. You should make clear that all words in the first column must have an *a* in the middle and all words in the third column an *i* in the middle. He can be introduced to the other columns (one at a time if you prefer) when he is ready for them.

He should also be encouraged to read downwards on some occasions, one column at a time; this will give him practice at reading the word 'in one', as opposed to sounding it out letter by letter, since this is easier when the vowel is unchanged.

After each vowel on p. 65 a number appears in brackets. This represents the order in which the short vowels should be taught, viz. *a*, *i*, *o*, *e*, *u*. The reason for this order is that one is thereby keeping separate the short *a* and the short *e* which are the two letters most easily confused. Many of the phonic readers mentioned on pp. 107–8 use this order.

The first page also contains the consonant digraphs *th*, *sh*, *ch*, and *wh*. Here the two letters together make a new sound, as if they were additional letters of the alphabet (compare p. 29). At a suitable point these four digraphs should be entered inside the cover. His attention should be called to the two slightly different ways of pronouncing *th*, as in *this* and *thin*.

Next come words ending in *-ng* and *-nk*, followed by some other

---

2. The symbol ˘ at the top of a vowel indicates the short sound, the symbol ‾ the long sound. Compare p. 34, footnote.

words which end in two consonants after a short vowel, viz. *-ll*, *-ff*, *-ss*, *-ch*, *-tch*, and *-dge*. These words require the inclusion of an extra letter in addition to what might be expected, either the same letter doubled or a related letter the addition of which is tantamount to doubling. Thus in *bell*, *off*, and *moss* the *l*, *f*, and *s* are simply doubled, while in the case of *sack*, *Scotch*, *bridge* a different letter is added, viz. a *c* before the *k*, a *t* before the *ch* and a *d* before the *ge*. *Kk* is never written but *c* is in effect a double to the *k*; the *t* in *-tch* is a substitute for a double since it would be cumbersome to write 'chch' and *t* is formed in the same place in the mouth as *ch* (something which the pupil can try out), while 'gege' would be similarly cumbersome and *d* is used because it is formed in the same place in the mouth as the soft *g* sound. However, as the use of *-ge* to represent this sound at the end of a word is not taught until Page 2 it is best to leave words in *-dge* until one is revising the Page 1 words and then add some of them to the list. The last two sentences in Exercise 1C have been designed to practise this ending.

Dyslexic children often have considerable difficulty with consonant blends (that is, consonants each of which has a separate sound). Some examples have been put inside the cover of the dictionary. In this case two or more sounds have to be blended together and the situation is different from that where the pairs of letters *ch*, *sh*, etc. are used to represent a single sound. When you practise these blends you should start with words having a short vowel sound and continue with other words as you move on to later pages in the dictionary. Games such as those mentioned in the previous chapter can be devised so as to give further practice. The most difficult blends are often ones with an *l* or *r* as second letter, for example *cl* and *pr*, and when three consonant sounds have to be blended, as in *spl*, *str*, etc., additional practice will almost certainly be necessary.

In Exercises 1B and 1C a few words have been introduced which end in a vowel, viz. *he*, *she*, *I*, *do* and *to*. At a later stage, when the pupil is aware of the difference between long and short vowels, you may like to call his attention to the fact that a vowel at the end of these words has a long and not a short sound; this is even true in some contexts of the word *the*, although quite often it is pronounced without a very specific vowel sound. For the present, however, we suggest that these five words are simply taken for granted, since they are usually known already.

The child should be told to begin every sentence in the exercises with a capital letter and end it with a full stop, unless, as in some sentences in Exercise 1C, he is learning to use a question mark or an exclamation mark.

This Page 1 work should not be covered too hastily. Progress at the beginning is slow; there is a whole new approach to be learned. It is boring to have to learn the same work over again because it was not sufficiently covered the first time. If necessary you should yourself invent further sentences for practising all the same points, and further sentences are also available in *Alpha to Omega* (for details see p. 111). Any word which has occurred once in the exercises may of course be used later for revision purposes.

Since different phonic readers differ as to which sounds they turn to next, we have tried to make the use of this book flexible at this point. Page 2 moves on to the long vowel/final *e* pattern, which fits with *Primary Phonics* and *More Primary Phonics*. But it is possible to do group (i) on Page 3 first, which is in line with the *Royal Road* series or group (ii) first which is in line with *One Way with Words* and also with *Alpha to Omega* (for further details of all these books see pp. 107–8, 111). Consequently Exercises 2A and 2B are independent of Exercises 3A and 3B and also of each other. By the time the pupil reaches Page 4 and its exercises it is assumed that all this ground has been covered.

Even when you move on past Page 1 you will regularly need to go back to it and remind the child of the words which it contains, perhaps at the beginning of each lesson.

The second page

To introduce this page you should begin by explaining the difference between long and short vowels. This can be done by means of examples, for example by telling him that $\breve{a}$ is a short sound and $\bar{a}$ a long one.[3] You can then test him by asking him to say 'short' or 'long' to the different sounds you make. The sound of a short vowel is, of course, clipped short as you speak it.

To make a long sound *two* vowels are needed. In the case of the sounds on this page the lengthening is achieved by adding an *e* (sometimes called 'silent *e*' or 'magic *e*') after the final consonant. Thus *mat* becomes *mate*, *bit* becomes *bite*, and *not* becomes *note*, the sound being the same as the name of the vowel.

At the top of the lists on Page 2 he should therefore write

| *a-e* | *e-e* | *i-e* | *o-e* | *u-e* |

In speech they should be called 'ā-blank-ē' or 'ā-consonant-ē'. The small dash between *a* and *e* etc. is for the consonant that goes in between, as in *game*, *ride*, and *rope*. The two vowels on either side of the consonant together make the long sound.

Although he should draw five columns on Page 2 it is better not to use the *e-e* and *u-e* columns at first. These two combinations are less common than the others, and you can come back and do them later (see the lists on p. 93). However, so that he can see that they work in the same way, we suggest that he writes just one word in each as an example, for instance *these* and *tune*. In all these cases the sound is also the name of the letter, although occasionally *u-e* is 'oo' rather than 'yoo'.

When you reach the later words on Page 2, such as *race* and *page*, this will probably be a convenient time for explaining when *c* and *g* are hard and soft, when to put -*ck* as opposed to *k*, and when to put -*dge* and -*tch* as opposed to -*ch*. The general rule is that *c* and *g* are hard before *a*, *o*, *u* and any consonant and soft before *e* and *i* (and before *y* when it is used as a vowel). You will, of course, need to show him by means of examples what you mean by 'hard' and 'soft' and indicate that the sounds of *s* and *j* are the same as the soft sounds of *c* and *g*. It will then be clear that if one puts an *e* after the *c* in words

3. Whether to teach the child the actual symbols, ˘ and ˉ, should be regarded as optional and should depend on what seems suitable in each case. If you wish the child to learn them we suggest that you give him a small piece of string: to make the sign for a short vowel he must curl the string up so that it is short; to make the sign for a long vowel he stretches it out so that it is as long as possible. *Space to Spell* (for details see p. 108) gives particularly useful practice at distinguishing between short and long vowel sounds.

such as *race*, *place*, etc. this gives the *c* an *s* sound, while if one puts an *e* after the *g* in words such as *page* and *stage* this gives the *g* a *j* sound. The *e* in such words in fact is doing two jobs, viz. making the vowel long and making the *c* or *g* soft. If a hard sound is needed before *e*, *i*, or *y* it is necessary to use *k* instead of *c* (as in *Kent* or *kill*), while if a soft sound is needed before *a*, *o* or *u* it is necessary to use *j* instead of *g* (as in *jam*, *job*, and *jug*). During his reading he may meet words such as *gentle*, *giant*, *gym*, *cell*, *city*, *cycle*. These are not words which he should attempt to spell at this stage, but they in fact follow the same principle, as do *guess*, *guilt*, and *guy* where a *u* is inserted after the *g* to make it hard. There are, however, a few common words which are exceptions, in particular *girl*, *get*, and *give*. These words come from Anglo-Saxon where the *g* is always hard. Welsh children sometimes find the *c/g* rule difficult to remember since in Welsh, as in Anglo-Saxon, *g* and *c* are always hard. Both Welsh and Scots Gaelic are Celtic languages (pronounced with a hard *c*), and it is a curiosity that because of the English rule the Scottish football club, Celtic, is universally pronounced with a soft *c*! Some of your brighter pupils may well be interested in points of this sort. The rule with regard to -*k* and -*ck* is that where there is a long vowel one uses -*k* and where there is a short vowel one uses -*ck*. Examples are *back/bake*, *duck/duke*, etc. Similarly one uses -*ch* and -*ge* at the end of a word when there is a long vowel immediately before the final consonant sound and -*tch* and -*dge* when there is a short vowel. This explains the spelling of *fetch*, *badge*, *wage*, etc.

At a suitable point the pupil should be encouraged to practise adding an *s* at the end of a word to make 'more than one'. This can be done both with Page 1 words (for example, *dogs*, *cats*) and with Page 2 words (for example *bones*, *cakes*). He should be asked to write the word in its singular form first and then think afterwards about adding the *s*. It is always an important principle that a dyslexic child should be asked to do *one thing at a time*; otherwise he becomes muddled between the two. He needs to follow the same practice later when adding -*ing* and -*ed* endings: he should write the base word first and afterwards think about the ending.

When 'more than one' is needed in the case of words ending in -*ss*, -*sh*, -*ch*, or -*x* one has to insert an *e* before adding the *s*, as in *crosses*, *brushes*, *benches*, and *foxes*. This is because we cannot pronounce such words without in effect adding a vowel. There are sentences at the end of Exercise 2B which practise this -*es* ending.

Like the words on Page 1, those on Page 2 will also need plenty of practice, again with extra sentences if you need them. Constant revision of Page 1 is also desirable so that the pupil can be reminded of the difference between the two pages.

The words at the bottom of the lists on Page 2 have been included so as to show the slightly different – and broader – sound of the vowel when an *r* is the consonant which comes between it and the final *e*, as in *bare, fire*, etc. Some of the readers which you will be using, for example Set 2, no. 10, in both *Primary Phonics* and *More Primary Phonics*, practise these long vowels with *r*. The ending -*ore*, as in *more*, has not been included because the sound is the same as that of *or* and is done with *or* on Page 3.

The third page

(i) The new sounds are again long vowel sounds, viz. *oo* (as in *moon* and *book*; the letters *oo* may stand for either) and *ee* (as in *green*). At this stage we suggest that you do not mention the other common way of spelling the long *e* sound, which is *ea* (as in *seat*). However we have taken care to include in the *ee* list some words which go easily together, viz. *green tree; see, seen, seem; meet in the street*, and *need sleep*, in the hope that these associations will still be remembered as indicating the *ee* pattern when the *ea* spelling is encountered later. Fortunately alternative ways of spelling the same sound as *oo* are more rare, viz. *ew* or *ue*; the pupil will not come across these for some time (compare p. 74).

(ii) The other sounds on Page 3 are not in fact two vowels at all but a single vowel with *r* added, viz. *ar, or*, and *er*. The sounds of these, however, are so different from the single vowel sound and the *r* is so little pronounced that they may almost be regarded as long vowel sounds.

The fourth page

When there is an *n* immediately before the last consonant of a word children often miss this out in spelling, probably because it can be heard only faintly, as a sort of grunt. If your pupil experiences this difficulty he should be told to listen very carefully and repeat the word to himself so as not to miss the 'grunting *n*'. There will be more 'grunting *n*' words later; for the present all the words in the list are short vowel words. One of them (*splint*) has three consonants at the beginning and these have to be picked out extra carefully. Exercises 4A and 4B practise these words and also, for the first time, introduce sounds from Pages 2 and 3 in the same sentences.

The fifth page

Some common irregular words are now introduced. They have been divided into twelve groups, the intention being that no more than one group need be learned at a time. A few of the words, for example, *is*, *go*, and *so*, have already appeared in the exercises; this is because they appear in early phonic readers and are likely to be known already. The others have been included in exercises from this point on so that they can be given regular practice.

As an aid to teaching irregular words, all unexpected or irregular letters have been underlined; and it is suggested that you should tell the pupil that these are the letters which need watching. For example *e* at the end of *are* and *have* does not in either case affect the sound, and the sound of the *a* in *was* is an unusual one. (Later in the programme you can point out that when the letter *a* appears after a *w* it is usually pronounced as if it were an *o*; see p. 73.) Similarly the letters *-ere* common to the three words in group (iii) are underlined, as are the letters *wh-* at the start of the question words in group (iv) and the letters *-se* at the end of the words in group (xi). The *ei* and *ey* patterns in *their* and *they* in group (vi) are similar to the *ai/ay* and *oi/oy* patterns on Pages 6, 7, and 8 in that *i* changes to *y* at the end of a word.

The sixth page

This introduces three sounds which come at the end of words, viz. *-ay* (as in *day*), *-oy* (as in *boy*) and *-y* (as in *my*).

In some cases new words can be formed by the addition of *-ing*, as in *playing*, *destroying* and *crying*. So that he does not have too much to do all at once he should be trained to write the base word first and add the *-ing* afterwards.

Words in group (vi) (Page 5) are included in Exercises 6A and 6B.

The long *a* sound is the same as that of *a-e* (Page 2) except that there is no consonant in between, as there is, for example, in the case of the word *gate*.

At the bottom of the *ay* column we have included two words in *ey*, viz. *they* and *grey*. The sound is the same as in *ay* but the written form *ey* is less frequent.

The seventh page

This page introduces *ai*, *ea*, and *oa*. These are sounds which the pupil has already met; but when he wrote them on Pages 2 and 3 he used the 'consonant-e' pattern, as in *late*, *these*, and *home*. (He will also have met the *ay* pattern for the long *a* sound, but this normally occurs only at the end of a word whereas the *ai* pattern is used in the middle and there need not therefore be any confusion.)

At this point there is the problem of remembering which words are spelled *a-e* and which are spelled *ai*, and similarly with the others. One way of helping is to put him on to readers where words having these new patterns are used, for example Set 2 no. 6 of *Primary Phonics* for *oa* words ('The Goat') and Set 2 no. 7 for *ai* words ('The Sail'). Remembering the story will help him to remember the different words in it which 'go the same way'; and it may be useful if he writes parts of the story down so that he is again working on the same words. A number of *ea* words, as it happens, have to do with food; and we sometimes tell our pupils a story about Jean who sat on a seat on the beach at the sea, eating a meal of meat, peas, and beans, followed by peaches and cream and a cup of weak tea.

Concluding remarks

From this point onwards it does not seem necessary to give detailed explanations page by page. Your basic procedure should continue to be the same as before: that is, you should gradually introduce new sounds, show the pupil the letters which represent these sounds and ask him to put the appropriate words into his dictionary; then you should work through the relevant exercise so that he has the chance both to practise these words (and others of a similar pattern) and to revise words whose patterns have already been shown to him. By all means invent your own sentences but make sure that you do not expect him to spell any word before you have explained its pattern. Words which are of a similar pattern to those already in the dictionary may be written in whenever you think he would find them interesting; for example the word *chain* could be added to Page 7 if he is interested in bicycles.

From Exercise 5 onwards the 'irregular' words on Page 5 are progressively introduced. Where appropriate an asterisked note has been used so as to remind you to introduce the relevant group(s) of words from Page 5 before starting the exercise.

With regard to the words on Page 11, it may be of help to invent 'silly sentences' so that the pupil can remember which words go *-aught* and which words go *-ought*. We have included one such sentence at the start of Exercise 11B, viz. 'I caught my naughty daughter and taught her not to slaughter'. We have also used 'I bought a football and brought it home,' 'I thought I ought to score a goal,' and 'I fought hard but I still got nought.'

When you introduce the words on Page 13 you should explain the 'doubling rule', viz. that the next consonant is doubled after a short vowel but remains single after a long vowel or pair of vowels, as in *kipper* and *wiper*, *hopping* and *hoping*, etc. After he is familiar with this rule you may like to return to the words in *-ck*, *-dge*, and *-tch* and explain how the addition of *c*, *d*, and *t* in these words was also a case of doubling or pseudo-doubling which is necessary whenever the previous vowel is short.

The doubling rule should also be mentioned when you introduce the words on Page 14. The pupil should note that when a word ends in *-ed* or *-ing* the previous vowel is long unless the consonant is doubled; for example the *o* in *hoping* is long while the *o* in *hopping* is short. When *-ed* or *-ing* are added to a word which ends in silent *e*, however, the silent *e* is no longer needed since the *-ed* and the *-ing* themselves make the vowel long and there is thus no need to retain the original final *e*. With regard to the words ending in *-y*, the main thing which needs to be remembered is that *y* usually changes to *i* in the middle of a word.[4] For this reason, when a past tense ending in -*ed* is needed, we write, for example, *tried* and *cried*, not 'tryed' and 'cryed'; and since in the case of the third person singular 'tris' and 'cris' would be odd, an *e* is inserted to give *tries* and *cries*. (The same thing also happens when a noun ending in *y* becomes plural, e.g. *berry*, *berries*.) When we need to add -*ing*, however, the writing of two consecutive *i*'s, as in 'triing' and 'criing', would be awkward, and the *y* is therefore retained so as to give *trying* and *crying*. Finally, if there is a vowel before it, the *y* is retained throughout; this means that we have, for example, *stay*, *stays*, *stayed*, *staying*, and *annoy*, *annoys*, *annoyed*, *annoying*. Similarly the plural of *abbey* is *abbeys*.[5]

When -*ly* is added to adjectives which already end in -*y* or -*ay* the first *y* changes to *i*, as in *happy*, *happily* and *gay*, *gaily*.

When you introduce the -*tion* words on Page 15 it is very important to get the pupil to count the number of syllables. A dyslexic person very easily 'loses the place', and unless he works out the separate parts of the word bit by bit there is a serious risk that he will put the letters in the wrong order. Some pupils may find it helpful to cover over the parts of the word which they are not looking at and even to say each part aloud so that they can make a comparison with the word which they are trying to spell. This can sometimes be a good way of helping a dyslexic person to monitor what he has written.

A page of 'extra words' has been included at the end. These are words which he is likely to need at some point but which have not been included in the programme. The words on this page and those in the supplementary word-lists in Appendix III can be taught as part of the programme if you wish, but it may be better to defer them until a later stage.

It is, of course, very important that as soon as possible every child

---

4. Words with *y* in the middle are rare in English. Those which occur have in many cases come into the language from Greek (compare the list on p. 97). The same Greek symbol has also been brought in as the common way of representing the long and short *i* sounds when they occur at the end of a word, and normally it is correct to put *i* in the middle of a word and *y* at the end.

5. If the pupil is interested in such matters you may like to point out to him that there are no nouns, verbs, or adjectives of English origin which have only two letters. The only two-letter words are words such as *by*, *in*, *am*, *as*, *if*, etc. This may explain why we write *lie*, *tie*, and *die* (not 'ly', 'ty' and 'dy'), whereas we do not write 'crie', 'drie', and 'trie' because *cry*, *dry*, and *try* already contain three letters.

should learn to read the words DANGER and POISON even if he cannot spell them.

Exercises 16A and 16B are not part of the programme but are designed to give practice at the spelling of words in Groups (iv) and (vi) of Appendix IV (for discussion see Chapter 6).

The material which we have suggested for inclusion in the dictionary will, we hope, be largely sufficient to give any child of average ability a sound basis for spelling such as would be possessed by the average nine-year-old. There is no reason why you should not push his reading level to a year or so ahead of his spelling level provided the gap is not so great that he loses contact between the two activities; what is important is that he should be encouraged to look at words carefully as he reads them, since once he acquires the habit of noticing detail there will be a corresponding improvement in his spelling.

Chapter 6

Word-endings and word-beginnings

Introduction

You may sometimes be in a position where you need to teach spelling to an older dyslexic child who is already familiar with most of the words in the basic programme. A good way of helping him is to call his attention to certain groups of letters which regularly occur as word-endings ('suffixes') or as word-beginnings ('prefixes'). If he is typically dyslexic, one of his great weaknesses is still likely to be his memory for sequences; and if he can become familiar with some of the standard combinations of letters and can be shown the reasons why a particular word is constructed as it is, the load on his memory will be correspondingly reduced.

The first part of this chapter will be concerned with word-endings – simpler ones in the first place and then harder ones – and the second part with word-beginnings. As a rough guide it is suggested that the simple word-endings should be given to pupils who are still of primary school age while the harder ones and the word-beginnings should be given to those aged eleven and over, since at this age they are likely to meet new subjects which have a technical vocabulary and are almost certain to make fresh demands in spelling. The exact pace at which you should go must of course depend on the needs of each individual child. Since some of the material, particularly the later sections, may seem formidable at first glance we should like to emphasize the importance of going slowly and of not presenting it in too large 'doses'.

At each stage the main text should be studied in conjunction with the word-lists in Appendix IV. We have not attempted in these lists to cover all possible words which the child could be expected to need; the appendix would in that case have been so complex as to be unusable, and we could justly have been accused of trying to imitate the White Knight, who, on the grounds that 'it's as well to be provided for *everything*', carried a mousetrap on his horse! In particular we decided that it was unnecessary to give comprehensive lists where some general rule was available, for example the rule that words ending in the -*ŭry* sound, if they are adjectives, are more likely to end -*ary* than -*ery*. Lists have been prepared only where there are no clear guide lines, for example in the case of words which could end either -*ent* or -*ant*. These lists can of course be added to whenever the child comes across other similar words which he needs to spell.

Only relatively few practice sentences have been provided (see Exercises 16A and 16B, p. 91). We thought that these would be helpful in the case of words ending in the *shun* sound (*suspicion*, *mention*, etc.) and also in the case of words ending in -*ous*, since for both sets of words the variations are somewhat complicated; and if the pupil has difficulty in remembering other endings you may wish to invent further sentences so as to give him the necessary practice. We are hesitant, however, to recommend extensive use of sentences at this stage of teaching. They do not help the pupil to appreciate good English and they limit him to specially selected words. Such limitation was necessary early on in his training because of the scarcity of words which he could then be expected to spell; but at an older age dictations involving unselected words are perhaps more appropriate.

Simpler word-endings ('suffixes')

We begin with the simpler endings, viz. -*y* and -*ey*, -*ed*, -*le* and -*el*, the *s* and *z* sounds at the end of a word, and -*ture*. The pupil will have met some of these when he was covering the basic programme, but we propose in what follows to go into somewhat more detail.

The -*y* and -*ey* endings

There are some words which sound as if they have a -*y* ending but whose spelling is *-ey*. These need to be specially noted, and a list of the more common ones has been provided in Appendix IV, Group (i), p. 99.

The -ed ending

In discussing the *-ed* ending you may like to return to p. 76 (Page 14 of the dictionary). The points to be noted are: (i) if the base word has a short vowel, then *two* consonants are needed before the *ed*, and if there was only one originally it has to be doubled. (ii) The *-ed* ending is normally required even in situations when the *-ed* sound is not heard; this can happen both when what is heard is a *t* sound and when the word is still of one syllable even when *-ed* has been added, as in *hope*, *hoped* and *stay*, *stayed*.

You may also wish to call attention to the small number of past tenses where the *t* sound is actually represented in the spelling. This can happen in particular when the present and past tenses have different vowel sounds, as in *sleep/slept*, *creep/crept*, *weep/wept*, and *mean/meant*.

There are also three irregular past tenses where *-ed* is not needed even though one would expect it from the sound; these are *pay/paid*, *lay/laid*, and *say/said*. The last of these, *said* (along with *says*), is also pronounced in an irregular way, and appears to be one of those everyday words which has been mauled in its pronunciation by constant use.

The -le and -el endings

-le is a very common ending for short words. Many of them are nouns, e.g. *table*, *bottle*; some are verbs, e.g. *nibble*, *hobble*, and a very few are adjectives, in particular *little*, *middle*, and *double*. The pronunciation is approximately '*ŭl*', and if the child is told that '*ŭl*' words normally end in *-le* he is unlikely to have any difficulty over the words on the list given in Appendix IV, Group (ii) (see p. 100). He may, however, need to be told that the rule about doubling the consonant after a short vowel applies in the case of these two-syllable words also, as, for instance, in *tāble* and *dabble*.

There are some words, however, which end in *-el*. Since they are much less common, it seems advisable not to start on them until the

-*le* words have been mastered. It is possible to give guidance as to which words go which way. This can be done as follows: words which have a 'hard' consonant or an *f* before the ending have -*le*, whereas words with a 'soft' consonant before the ending have -*el*. The 'hard' consonants are *b*, *p*, *d*, *t*, *k*, hard *c* and hard *g*; the 'soft' ones are *ss*, *v*, *w*, *m*, *n*, soft *c*, and soft *g*. The child will already have met the difference between 'hard' and 'soft' *c* and *g* (p. 34), and will now be able to see that, in general, *ss*, *v*, *w*, *m*, and *n* make softer sounds than *b*, *p*, *d*, and *t*. After a hard consonant and an *f* the letter *l* (pronounced '*ŭl*') is much easier to say than after soft consonants, and it can follow the consonant immediately with no difficulty in pronunciation; when the '*ŭl*' sound follows a soft consonant, however, pronunciation is difficult unless a vowel sound comes in between, which is why the *e* comes first when the consonant is soft. If the child is asked to say *table* and *towel* successively the difference will probably become clear to him. With soft *c* and soft *g* (as in *parcel* and *angel*) there must in any case be an *e* immediately afterwards to ensure that the *c* and *g* remain soft. The words on p. 100 have therefore been arranged to show the division between hard consonants and *f* (with -*le*) on the one hand and soft consonants (with -*el*) on the other. Below these two main lists we have given a list of the very few exceptions.

The *s* and *z* sounds may cause some doubt. Double *z* counts as a hard letter, as in *dazzle*, while double *s* is clearly soft, as in *tassel* and *vessel*. Where the *s* is followed by a silent *c* or *t* (as in *muscle* and *castle*) the spelling is -*le*, in deference, as it were, to the hard letters which are present but not pronounced. Where there is a single *z* or an *s* pronounced as a *z*, however, the spelling, surprisingly, is -*el*, as in *hazel* and *easel*. (The only common exception to this is *measles*.) We are not, of course, talking here about words where the emphasis is on the -*el* ending, such as *hotél* and *expél*; no rules are needed for words of this kind, since the spelling must clearly be -*el* because of the sound.

A very common -*le* ending is -*able*, as in *probable*; also quite a number of words end in -*ible*, e.g. *possible*. In these cases we cannot hear the vowel distinctly because the emphasis is on the beginning of the word; we cannot therefore go by what we hear but must simply bear in mind that the *ŭble* sound is much more often spelled -*able* than -*ible*. It is the -*ible* words, therefore, which have to be remembered specially and a list of the most common is to be found in Appendix IV, Group (ii), p. 101.

The s and z sound at the end of a word

To introduce these sounds you may find it helpful to call the child's attention to the fact that, although regular plurals simply involve the addition of *s*, this *s* is sometimes pronounced as though it were a *z*; thus although the plural of *clock*, *clocks*, has an *s* sound, the plural of *hen*, *hens*, has a *z* sound. Similarly the third-person singular of verbs is always spelled with *s* but is sometimes pronounced as though the *s* were a *z*, as in *begs*.

On other occasions when an *s* or *z* sound is heard, it is rarely spelled just *s* or just *z*. The following rules usually apply:

(i) If the *s* sound follows a short vowel the spelling is usually -*ss* (double *s*), as in *less*, *kiss*, and *toss*. (The only common words having the *s* sound and yet ending in single *s* are *gas*, *atlas*, *Christmas*, *this*, *thus*, *bus*, *plus*, and *minus*.)

(ii) If the *s* sound follows a long vowel or pair of vowels, the spelling at the end of the word will be either -*ce*, as in *face* and *peace*, or -*se* as in *case* and *house*.

(iii) If the *z* sound follows a short vowel, then the *z* is doubled, as *fizz*.

(iv) If the *z* sound follows a long vowel or pair of vowels, the spelling at the end of the word will be either -*ze*, as in *prize* and *freeze*, or -*se* as in *rise* and *choose*.

In brief, apart from plurals and the third-person singular of verbs, if there is an *s* sound at the end of the word one writes either -*se* or -*ce*; if there is a *z* sound one writes either -*se* or -*ze*. No attempt has been made to list all the words which exemplify this principle, since this would have made the appendix too unwieldy.

It is also worth remembering that there are many longer words having the *s* sound which end in -*ence* and -*ance*, such as *convenience* and *importance*. These are discussed on p. 53.

The -ture ending

This ending is pronounced approximately '*cher*', and the pupil can be told that to represent the '*cher*' sound the spelling *-ture* is most usual.

There are, however, a few words which end in the '*cher*' sound, but are spelled exactly as they sound. Among the commonest are: *teacher*, *preacher*, *butcher*, *archer*, *stretcher*, and *voucher*. Others will be found to derive from a verb ending in *-ch*, with the additional *-er* representing the person who does the activity in question, e.g. *poach*, *poacher*.

A list of words ending in *-ture* is given in Appendix IV, Group (iii), p. 101.

Harder word-endings

We shall begin by considering words with the '*shun*' ending, after which we shall take in order the following endings: *-age*, *-ace*, and *-ate*; *-ous*; *-al*; *-ery* and *-ary*; *-ent* and *-ant*; and *-ence* and *-ance*.

The 'shun' *ending*

Once a pupil is familiar with the combination *-tion* he should be encouraged, when he needs to spell longer words, to listen for the sound *immediately before* the ending. In many cases this is a vowel, as in *indignation*, *commotion*, etc., and he is unlikely to have any problem in determining which vowel it is.

If it is a consonant, however, this may be more difficult, since consonants tend to combine with the *sh* sound in ways which may be unfamiliar to him. The important combinations are *-ption* (as in *adoption*), *-ction* (as in *fiction*), *-stion* (as in *question*), *-ntion* (as in *mention*), and – most difficult of all – *-nction* (as in *junction*). Considerable practice may be needed before the pupil can pick out these combinations and letters every time. When he is able to do so, he will be able to pay more attention to the earlier syllables. This is again one of the situations where he should be asked to count the number of syllables so as to make sure none are added or omitted (compare p. 40).

There is a further complication which awaits the pupil when he has reached a more advanced stage: the same *shun* -sound can be spelled in other ways, viz. -*cion*, -*sion*, and -*ssion*. Lists of words with these different endings are given in the Appendix IV, Group (iv), p. 102.

Words in -cion
Fortunately *there are only two words in -cion*, viz. *suspicion* and *coercion*; and these can therefore be learned individually.

Words in -shion
Similarly there are only two words in -*shion*, viz. *cushion* and *fashion*, and these can also be learned individually.

Words in -sion
With regard to -*sion*, the following guide-lines apply: (i) after *l* one finds only -*sion*, as in *compulsion*; (ii) after *n* or *r* one finds both -*sion* and -*tion*, as in *tension*, *version*, *attention*, *exertion*, etc., and a list of the most common words of each kind has therefore been provided on p. 102; (iii) where there is a '*zhun*' sound after a vowel, the correct spelling is always -*sion*, as in *occasion* and *cohesion*.

Words in -ssion
The common -*ssion* words have been listed on p. 102.
Sentences have been provided on p. 91 so as to give the pupil practice at recognizing these somewhat complex differences.

The -age, -ace, -ate endings

These three endings illustrate the fact that the last syllable in some English words is not fully pronounced, as in *damage*, *menace*, and *fortunate*. The sounds are approximately '*ŭj*' or '*ĭj*', '*ŭs*', and '*ŭt*', but from these on their own it is not clear what vowel is needed.

The following guide-lines may be helpful: (i) nouns whose ending sounds like '*ŭj*' or '*ĭj*' often end in -*age*; (ii) nouns whose ending sounds like '*ŭs*' often end in -*ace*; (iii) adjectives whose ending sounds like '*ŭt*' often end in -*ate*. Lists of words with these endings are given in Appendix IV, Group (v), p. 103.

Verbs ending in -*ate* are easier to deal with, since the long *a* is clearly sounded, as in *excavate*.

The -ous ending

The ending *-ous* has much the same sound as the ending *-ace*. While most *-ace* words are nouns, however, most *-ous* words are adjectives.

In Appendix IV, Group (vi), p. 104, these adjectives have been classified into various groups. Words with a consonant before the *-ous* are the most straightforward, e.g. *famous*, and we have included in this list two words in *-geous* (*gorgeous* and *courageous*) where the function of the *e* before the *-ous* is simply to soften the *g* and is not heard. Where there is an *ĭ* sound (short *i*), before the *-ous*, *-ious* is likely to be right more often than *-eous*, but words with both kinds of ending have been listed for reference.

In the case of adjectives ending in *-tious* and *-cious* it may be helpful to draw a comparison with words which end *-tion* and *-cion*. Here the *ti* and *ci* are both ways of spelling the *sh* sound; and in the same way, if an adjective ending in *-ous* has this *sh* sound, the spelling is likely to be either *-tious* or *-cious*. *-cious* is in fact much more common than *-cion*, and of the adjectives which end in *-tious* (as opposed to *-cious*) the great majority are connected with a *-tion* noun; *ambitious*, for example, is connected with *ambition*.

If there is an *n* sound before the *-shus* the word will always end *-tious*, as in *pretentious* or *licentious*.

If a *k* sound occurs immediately before the *sh* sound this *k* sound may combine with the *s* sound to form an *x* and we will get *xi*. The child who understands this point can therefore be warned to expect some words to end in *-xious*, the two main ones being *anxious* and *noxious*. He should remember, however, that *infectious* keeps the *-cti*, since it follows the related noun, *infection*.

Sentences for practice are given on p. 91.

The -al ending

It is useful to leave an appreciable gap between doing the *-le/-el* endings (pp. 45–7 above) and doing words in *-al*, so as to avoid possible confusion between the two.

Most *-le* and *-el* words are nouns; in contrast words ending in *-al* are mainly adjectives. Thus if a word with the *ŭl* sound at the end is an adjective there is a good chance that the spelling *-al* will be correct, as in *usual* or *original*. This general rule covers so many adjectives that it seemed to us unnecessary to list them separately in the Appendix. The only major group of exceptions are adjectives ending in *-able* or *-ible*, e.g. *portable* and *possible*.

In the case of nouns having the *ŭl* sound, however, the position is more complicated. Where the spelling is *-al*, these nouns can conveniently be divided into two classes:

(i) There are some nouns which are derived from verbs, e.g. *trial*, *denial*, *rehearsal*, *betrayal*. These are instantly recognizable from the fact that, when the *ŭl* sound is removed, a familiar verb is left, viz. *try*, *deny*, *rehearse*, *betray*. These words can helpfully be included in the pupil's notebook.

(ii) Quite a number of nouns in *-al* are also used as adjectives. In some cases both noun and adjective are likely to be familiar to the pupil, e.g. *general*, *corporal*, *material*, *moral*. There are other words, however, where the adjectival usage is not very common; thus the word *animal* is an adjective in the expression 'animal behaviour' and the word *signal* is an adjective in the expression 'a signal success'. One must assume that only the very bright pupils will recognize the adjectival usage in these less obvious cases. In spite of this, however, it seemed to us helpful to collect together in the Appendix all the *-al* nouns which can function as adjectives (see Appendix IV, Group (vii), p. 105); then if the pupil *knows* that they are also adjectives he will not need to learn them separately. Words in the list can then be distinguished from *-al* nouns which *never* function as adjectives, e.g. *sandal*, *rascal*, where the *-al* ending simply has to be learned. There seems no reason, for example, why *sandal* should be spelled *-al* and *candle -le*. Nouns in *-al* are, of course, far less numerous than nouns in *-le*.

A word which may cause special trouble is the word *principal*. Not only can it be both a noun (e.g. the principal of a college) and an adjective (meaning 'chief'); it is also liable to be confused with the *-le* noun, *principle*, which means approximately 'rule'.

In the case of adjectives having the *shŭl* sound at the end, e.g. *initial* and *crucial*, there is no means of knowing whether the spelling should be *-tial* or *-cial*. If the pupil is in doubt he has a better chance of success if he puts *-tial*, since *-tial* words are the more common, while if there is an *n* before the *shŭl* sound, the spelling will almost certainly be *-tial*, as in *essential*, *influential*, and *torrential*. (A helpful comparison can be made here with the *shŭs* sound: when there is an *n* before this sound, the spelling is almost certain to be *-tious*, not *-cious*, as in *pretentious*, see p. 50.) We have found two exceptions to this rule, viz. *financial* and *provincial*; despite the *n* before the *shŭl* sound both these words end in *-cial*.

The -ery and -ary, -ent and -ant, and -ence and -ance endings

In saying words of this kind one makes the somewhat 'nondescript' sounds '*ŭry*', '*ŭnt*', and '*ŭnce*' with no clearly recognizable vowel. The following suggestions, however, may help the pupil to decide whether this 'nondescript' sound should be represented by *e* or *a*.

Words in -ery

(i) *Many words in -ery* express a sort of stock-in-trade of a trader, and the pupil will already know that the word for a person who 'does something' (such as trading) is likely to end in *-er*. Thus we have:

grocer – grocery
stationer – stationery (notepaper, etc.)
cutler – cutlery
collier – colliery
robber – robbery

Also, even when there is not a word ending in *-er* for the 'agent', there may still be a reference to stock-in-trade or 'doing something' which justifies the use of *-ery*; thus we have *embroidery*, *trickery*, *foolery*, *finery*, *mockery*, *cookery*, *bribery*, and *machinery*.

(ii) Where a word refers to a place of some kind *-ery* is the more likely ending, as in *gallery*, *shrubbery*, *rockery*, *Chancery*, *Deanery*, *nursery*, and *cemetery*.

(iii) There are adjectives in *-ery* which are connected with nouns in *-er*. Some of the more common ones are: *powdery*, *papery*, *feathery*, *coppery*, *silvery*, *thundery*, *watery*, and *peppery*. These adjectives mean 'like powder', 'like paper', etc. You may also like to call the pupil's attention to *fiery* which is unexpected.

Words in -ary

Where the word is an adjective the ending *-ary* is far more likely than the ending *-ery*, as in *imaginary*, *necessary*, and *stationary* (in the sense of 'not moving').

There are also a few nouns which end in *-ary*, in particular *dictionary*, *boundary*, *constabulary*, and *dromedary*.

In some cases the pupil may be able to discover the correct vowel in an *ŭry* word by trying to find a connected word in which the vowel sound is clear. Thus *imaginary* is connected with *imagination*, where the *ā* sound (long *a*) stands out; similarly *history* must be *-ory* because in the word *historian* an *o* is clearly heard (compare also *category*, *memory*, and *allegory*). By the same argument *stationery* (in the sense of 'note-paper') must end *-ery*, since *stationer* ends in *-er*.

All the above words can helpfully be included in the pupil's notebook.

Words in -ent and -ant

The rule about hard and soft *g* and *c* (p. 34) is of help in some cases: thus where there is hard *g* or hard *c* one can expect the ending *-ant*, as in *elegant*, *extravagant*, *significant*, and *applicant*, and where there is a soft *g* or soft *c* one can expect *-ent* (with the *e* keeping the *g* or *c* soft), as in *indulgent*, *intelligent*, *recent*, and *innocent*. (Very occasionally you may meet a word with a soft *g* which nevertheless ends in *-ant*, e.g. *pageant* and *sergeant*, and in these cases, of course, an *e* is needed after the *g* to keep it soft). The *s-* and *sh* sounds go the same way as the soft *c* sound and therefore require *-ent*, as in *effervescent*, *patient*, and *efficient*. *-ment* is a particularly common ending for nouns derived from verbs, e.g. *excitement* and *amusement*.

Words in -ence and -ance

The same principles apply in the case of words ending in *-ence* and *-ance*. The following may be cited as examples of words which obey the rule about hard and soft *g* or *c*: *elegance*, *significance*, *intelligence*, and *adolescence*. Similarly where there is an *s* or *sh* sound the spelling is likely to be *-ence*, as in *essence* and *conscience*.

In the case of other words in this group there seems no alternative other than gradually learning them from the lists. Some of the more common nouns and adjectives in *-ent* and *-ant* are therefore set out in Appendix IV, Group (viii), p. 106.

Word-beginnings ('prefixes')

The lists which follow contain some of the more common prefixes. They include both those which stay the same whatever letter comes afterwards and others where the final consonant may be affected by the next letter in the word; thus the prefix *circum-* never changes, while the prefix *con-* changes to *m* before a *p* or *b*, as in *compare* and *combine*. Our suggestion is that the pupil should learn these prefixes in such a way that he can recognize them at once when he reads them; and he can then set off confidently, because of their familiarity, when he has to spell a word which begins with one of them.

When the changes mentioned above occur the result is sometimes a double consonant, as in *commit*, *difficult*, and *appear*. This, however, is not true doubling such as we have come across earlier in connection with short vowels, for the very good reason that no extra letter has been added. What happens is that the final consonant of the prefix is *assimilated* to the beginning consonant of the next part of the word. The presence of a short vowel in the prefix does not on its own necessitate a double letter, as can be seen from some of the words in the list of *pre-*, *de-*, *re-*, and *pro-* prefixes below.

We have not included the basic meaning of these prefixes in the present chapter nor any derivations, whether from Latin, Greek, or Anglo-Saxon. To do so usually creates only an extra complication. When a prefix occurs in a compound word, its meaning as part of the compound may not be at all near its original meaning; for example, the word *announce* involves the prefix *ad-*, but a knowledge that 'ad' in Latin means 'towards' does not help a dyslexic child to spell the word correctly. What is needed is *recognition* of prefixes for spelling purposes, and this can be taught without troubling the pupil about their meanings. If, however, the teacher wishes to make a more systematic study of prefixes in general and what they mean, a comprehensive list will be found in *Chambers Twentieth Century Dictionary*.

We are assuming that the pupil is aged thirteen or more by the time he has reached this point and that he is capable of reasonably advanced work, e.g. CSE or O level English.

The prefixes circum-, inter-, mis-, per- and contra-

These prefixes never change. Some of the more common words having these prefixes are:

circumstance	interval	mistake	perfect	contradict
circumference	interlude	misfire	permit	contravene
circumscribe	interview	misunderstand	perfume	
circumspect	interpreter	misplace	perform	
circumvent	interloper	misbehave	percussion	

It should be noted that the prefix *mis-* has only one *s* unlike the short words of similar sound, e.g. *miss*, *kiss*, and *bliss*; it is helpful to remember that *-ss* is an ending.

The prefixes pre-, de-, re-, and pro-

These prefixes also never change. Some of the more common words having these prefixes are:

prefect	decide	report	progress
prepare	depart	remark	pronoun
prefix	deceive	reward	product
preposition	detail	return	profess
prefer	determine	restrain	profit

These prefixes are awkward in that the sound of the word as spoken does not always indicate clearly what is the right vowel to use. Sometimes the sound is $\bar{e}$ (long *e*), or $\bar{o}$ (long *o*), as in *prefix* and *pronoun*; sometimes it is $\breve{e}$ (short *e*) or $\breve{o}$ (short *o*), as in *preposition* and *profit*. It seems best, therefore, that the pupil should learn the spelling of these prefixes rather than try to infer it from the sound.

The prefixes en-, in-, con-, and syn-

These can be grouped together because they all end in *n*. Usually the *n* stays, but before *b* or *p* it changes to *m*, and (except in the case of *en-*) it also changes to *m* before another *m*. Examples are as follows:

Stays the same	*Changes*
engage	embrace
	emperor
inactive	imbibe
invade	important
	immense
confident	combine
conclude	company
	commit
syntax	symbol
	sympathy
	symmetry

In the case of *in-* and *con-* before *l* and *r*, there is assimilation of the consonant, as in *illegal*, *irrigation*, *collect* and *correct*. *syn-* gives double *l* (as in *syllable*) but there is no case of double *r*.

The prefixes dis- and ex-

These can be grouped together because of the *s* sound at the end. Both of them stay the same before most letters but when the next part of the word begins with an *f* there is assimilation and the correct spelling is *-ff* (double *f*). Examples are as follows:

Stays the same	*Changes*
disappoint	difficult
dislike	different
exit	effort
expel	effect

However there are also the forms *di-* and *e-* which are unchanging like the prefixes *cirum-*, *inter-*, etc.

diverse	emit
dilate	evade

The prefix *dys-* is rare. Its general sense is 'difficulty with'; thus a person with *dyspepsia* has difficulty with digestion. This prefix would barely be worth mentioning were it not for the fact that the pupil may sometimes need to know how to spell *dyslexia*!

The prefixes sub- and ob-

These remain the same except when followed by *c*, *f*, *p*, and (in the case of *sub-*) *g*. In these cases there is assimilation and the consonant doubles. Examples of both types are as follows:

Stays the same	*Changes*
suburb	succeed, success, occupy
subway	suggest, suggestion
subsidence	suffer, offer
object	sufficient
obstruct	suppose, opposite
	support
	supply

There is not usually any change when *sub-* and *ob-* are followed by the letter *m*, as in *sub*marine. In some words which start *summ-* (e.g. *summary*, *summit*), this double *m* is not caused by the prefix *sub-* which is not present in these words, though it is present in the case of the word *summon*.

The prefix ad-

This prefix stays the same before vowels and before *h*, *j*, *m*, and *v*, and there is usually doubling of the consonant before *b*, *c*, *d*, *g*, *l*, *n*, *r*, *s*, and *t*. Examples are as follows:

Stays the same	*Changes*
adapt	abbreviate
adept	accord, accept, access, accent
adopt	affect, afflict, affair, affirm
	aggressive, aggregate
adhere	allow, allotment, allocate
adjective	announce, annoy
admit	arrest, arrive, arrange
advice	assert, assist
	attend, attach, attempt, attack

Ad- before a *q* becomes *acq-*, as in *acquaint*, *acquiesce*, *acquire*, and *acquit*.

Where there is no doubling of the consonant (as in *abroad*, *aloft*, *ablaze*, and *abreast*), this is because the word does not have the prefix *ad-* but the less common one, *a-*. It will be noticed that these four words (unlike the ones given above) would still be complete words even if the *a* at the start were taken away; this confirms that no assimilation has taken place.

To call the pupil's attention to word-endings and word-beginnings is one way of encouraging him to look at words *in detail*. If he cannot absorb the whole word at once it is clearly better that he should break it down into manageable parts rather than make a wild guess.

Chapter 7

Help with Arithmetic

Many dyslexic children have problems with arithmetic. This is an area which requires considerable further investigation, and in this chapter we shall limit ourselves to describing some of the difficulties and making a few somewhat tentative suggestions.

We have found it important, in the first place, to call the child's attention to the difference between mathematics on the one hand and arithmetic (or calculation) on the other. It should be made clear to him that a dyslexic person may quite often be able to grasp abstract and complicated mathematical ideas and yet have difficulty over what seem to the rest of us to be simple calculations. Just because he is worse than many of his classmates over calculation, therefore, he should not conclude that he is 'no good at maths'. We know, in fact, of a university lecturer in physics (a subject which needs mathematics of a very high order) who still needs to use his fingers for subtraction and cannot always give the answer to simple multiplication sums (e.g. 'six times seven') without the use of some sort of compensatory strategy.

The three most common arithmetical difficulties which we have met in dyslexic children are (a) difficulty over simple addition and subtraction, (b) difficulty in learning tables by rote, and (c) difficulties arising from uncertainty over direction both in space and time.

(a) There are some dyslexic children who cannot do addition and subtraction unless they provide for themselves a visible or tangible representation of the numbers involved. If the number to be added or subtracted is very small, for example 2 or 3, they can usually give the correct answer instantly, but if higher numbers are involved they appear to need compensatory strategies, many of which they may have devised for themselves. For example, if the sum is 44−7, we have met children who have divided up the 7 into 4 and 3 (an operation which is within the limits of what they can manage); they then use 40 as an 'anchor point' and count back the remaining three numbers one by one so as to arrive correctly at 37. If the sum is 19−7 we have met children who carefully write 19 tallies on the page, cross off 7 of them and count the remainder – a time-consuming procedure and one which can sometimes lead to an error of at least one in either direction. Other children use their fingers, and some years ago one of us tested a girl who said that she had been reprimanded for using her fingers and therefore used her toes!

(b) When dyslexic children are asked to say their tables aloud they are liable to lose the place or break into the 'wrong' table. For example they might go correctly as far as 'four sixes are twenty four', pause, murmur 'six sixes', and then ask, 'Was it five sixes I was up to?' If told to learn tables by heart many of them find the task virtually impossible.

(c) There are a number of difficulties which arise as a result of uncertainty over direction in space and time. Memorizing the order in which operations are to be performed may not be easy. Similarly they may see the figures '16' and think to themselves (or say aloud) 'sixty-one'. They may start a subtraction sum on the left when they should have started on the right or confuse units, tens, and hundreds through not shifting one column to the left at the correct time. They may also have difficulty in converting figures into words and vice versa, for example 'one thousand three hundred and twenty seven' might be written as 100030027 (which is logical enough but happens to be wrong). There may also be difficulties over the 'greater than' and 'less than' symbols and, in more advanced work, over symbols which express direction of flow.

At present too little research has been done for us to be sure of the most effective ways of compensating for these deficiencies. We suggest, therefore, that you encourage the pupil to try out some of the procedures which follow and that he should select those which he finds most helpful.

(a) With regard to difficulties over addition and subtraction, the important thing in the first place is to be sure that he understands basic principles, for example what is involved in adding on or in taking something away from something else. You should check that he knows that 'plus' and '+' mean the same as 'add' and that 'minus' and '−' mean the same as 'subtract' or 'take away'. You should check that after adding or taking away he can correctly use the terms 'more' and 'less' and that he knows that 9, for example, is more than 5 and that 22 is more than 19. You should also check that he understands about 'place value', that is, that the figure on the right represents units, the figure next to it on the left represents tens, and so on. There may well be features in the notation of our number system that he has failed to 'pick up' in the normal way.

He may well be helped if adding and taking away are illustrated in 'concrete' fashion with the aid of blocks or beads. He can be asked to carry out the actual operations of adding a specified number of objects to those already in a pile or taking a specified number away. If the numbers involved are more than about five he may like to break them down into smaller numbers. For example it would probably not take him long to learn that $6 = 3 + 3, 7 = 4 + 3, 8 = 4 + 4$, and $9 = 5 + 4$. When he has to take away 6, 7, 8, or 9 he will then be in a position to carry out the operation in two successive stages rather than run the risk of 'losing his place' by attempting a single operation. Since dyslexia regularly involves problems of immediate memory, he should be encouraged to write the numbers down so that he can tell at once the stage of the operation which he has reached.

(b) With regard to tables, an obvious aid is to show him how to use a table-square. This is simply a sheet of paper with the numbers 1 to 12 running across and vertically and the products set out as we have indicated below:

1	2	3	4	5	6	7	8	9	10	11	12
2	4	6	8	10	12	14	16	18	20	22	24
3	6	9	12	15	18	21	24	27	30	33	36
4	8	12	16	20	24	28	32	36	40	44	48
5	10	15	20	25	30	35	40	45	50	55	60
6	12	18	24	30	36	42	48	54	60	66	72
7	14	21	28	35	42	49	56	63	70	77	84
8	16	24	32	40	48	56	64	72	80	88	96
9	18	27	36	45	54	63	72	81	90	99	108
10	20	30	40	50	60	70	80	90	100	110	120
11	22	33	44	55	66	77	88	99	110	121	132
12	24	36	48	60	72	84	96	108	120	132	144

To determine 7 × 8, for example, he moves horizontally until he reaches the 7, moves downwards in the left-hand column until he reaches 8 and looks at the point where the 7 column and the 8 row intersect. (Describing this procedure in words is somewhat complicated but if you *show* him what is involved, he is unlikely to have any difficulty.)

In point of fact the 5, 10, and 11 times tables do not involve a heavy load on the memory for obvious reasons and he is likely to be able to learn these without recourse to the table-square. He can also be told that in the case of the 9 times the figure on the left decreases by 1 each time and that the two figures together add up to 9.

If he is interested you may like to show him how to do 'finger multiplication'.[1] We have not tried it out systematically ourselves, but we have been told of children who have benefited from it. The hands are held out with palms facing each other. The thumb of each hand is made to represent the number 6, the index finger the number 7, the middle finger the number 8, the fourth finger the number 9, and the fifth finger the number 10. Figure 6 shows a left and right hand with the number attached to each.

If the sum is 8 × 7, the third finger of one hand (representing 8) is placed against the index finger of the other hand (representing 7). The figure for the tens column of the answer is given by counting the

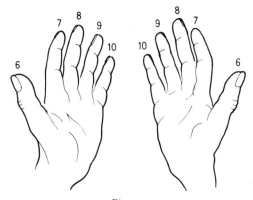

Fig. 6

1. We are grateful to Mrs Jill Playford, of the Helen Arkell Centre, London, for showing us this method.

number of fingers on the body-side of the point of contact (including the two fingers which are touching), in this case 5; the figure for the units column is obtained by multiplying the number of 'remaining fingers' on one side by the number of 'remaining fingers' on the other, in this case 2 × 3 = 6, and the answer is therefore 56. No knowledge of any table beyond the 4 times is needed and the amount of counting, with resultant risk to a dyslexic child of losing the place, is very limited. There is a complication in that 6 × 6 has to be calculated as 20 + 16 and 7 × 6 as 30 + 12, but for all other products the multiplying together of the 'remaining fingers' gives a number less than 10 and no carrying from the units column is needed.

(c) With regard to difficulties over direction, we suggest regular practice with the terms 'left' and 'right', 'up' and 'down', and 'before' and 'after'. Such practice can be 'multisensory' in character. Not only can the pupil be asked to listen to successive sounds so as to become sure of the words 'before' and 'after', but he can learn to describe the relative position of symbols and objects on the page ('the 6 is to the right of the 9', 'the chair is to the left of the table', etc.), and he can move his own hands or body from left to right or from right to left. Many dyslexic children have learned compensatory devices by which they can tell which are their right and left hands, and it will help them in general if you make explicit that a word or symbol on the *right* of the page often needs to be thought of as coming *after* one on the left.

Finally, if a dyslexic pupil is taking an examination which involves calculation he should be encouraged to take his time, to proceed step by step, and not to panic. Some preliminary practice at doing arithmetical calculations under pressure of time may serve to acclimatize him to the examination atmosphere. He should also be advised to read the question very carefully, and not mistake, for example, 'greater than' for 'less than' or leave out important symbols such as the square root sign.

In general it seems safe to say that difficulties over calculation can be a nuisance but need not be an insuperable obstacle which prevents progress in mathematics. Here, as in many other areas, it is perfectly possible for a dyslexic person to achieve success.

Appendix I   A sample dictionary

INSIDE COVER OF DICTIONARY

VOWELS

a e i o u   y

A E I O U   Y

CONSONANTS

b c d f g h j k l m n p qᵘ r s t v w x y z

B C D F G H J K L M N P Qu R S T V W X Y Z

| th | sh | ch | wh | | ph |

bl   cr   st

-ng   -nk

-ll   -ff   -ss   -ck   -tch   -dge

Page 1

	a (1)*	*e* (4)	*i* (2)	*o* (3)	*u* (5)
(i)	cat	hen	pig	dog	cup
	man	bed	hit	top	sun
	bag	leg	lid	fox	hut
(ii)	bash	shed	ship	shop	shut
	dash		fish	posh	rush
	that	then	this	moth	thug
			with		
	chat	chest	chip	chop	chug
		when			
	sang		sing	song	sung
	tank		pink	honk	trunk
(iii)	shall	bell	hill	doll	gull
			cliff	off	cuff
		mess	kiss	moss	fuss
	sack	deck	pick	rock	duck
	black	peck	stick	clock	stuck
	catch	fetch	witch	Scotch	hutch
	patch	ketchup	pitch		
	badge	hedge	bridge	dodge	budge
		edge	fridge	lodge	fudge

Notes
1. Leave the -*dge* ending until you have done -*ge* on Page 2.
2. *Much*, *rich*, *such*, and *which* do not have a *t*.

* The numbers after each vowel indicate the order in which the sounds should initially be learned (see p. 31).

Page 2

a-e	e-e	i-e	o-e	u-e
late	these	time	home	tune
take		nine	bone	
cake		pipe	rope	
came		like	joke	
made		five	nose	
gave		ride	rode	
race		quite	stove	
place		pile	hole	
page		nice		
bare		fire		

Page 3

(i)

oo	*ee*
moon	green
food	tree
boot	see seen seem
spoon	been (be)
tool	meet (run into)
too	street
	queen
book	need
look	sleep
cook	sheep
good	week (7 days)

(ii)

ar	*or(e)*	*er*
car	or	her
far	for	un'der
farm	fork	sis'ter
hard	corn	win'ter
dark	short	term
barn	more	perch
start	score	

Page 4

-ng, -nk, -nd, and -nt

bang		bring	long
sang		sing	song
thank		wink		bunk
drank		drink		drunk
hand	mend		pond	fund
sand	spend			
pant	bent	mint		shunt
	lent	splint		blunt

Page 5

Irregular words

(i)   is   ar_e_
       w_a_s   wer_e_

(ii)   hav_e_
        giv_e_
        liv_e_

(iii)   h_e_re
         th_e_re
         wh_e_re

(iv)   _wh_en
        _wh_ich (no *t*)
        _wh_at
        _wh_ere
        _wh_y
        _wh_o

(v)   no
       go
       so
       do

(vi)   I   my
        he   his
        she   her
        it   its
        we   our
        y_ou_   y_ou_r
                 (you + r)
        they   th_ei_r

(vii)   (*o* = short *u*, sometimes
          with extra *e*)

m_o_ther	c_o_m_e_	s_o_n
br_o_ther	s_o_m_e_	fr_o_nt
_o_ther	d_o_n_e_	_o_n_e_
an_o_ther	l_o_v_e_	_o_nc_e_
n_o_thing	ab_o_v_e_	L_o_nd_o_n

(viii)   t_wo_
          three
          f_our_ (4 letters)
          five
          six

(ix)   Mr
        Mrs
        said
        saw
        father

(x)   coul_d_
       woul_d_
       shoul_d_

(xi)   _a_ny
        m_a_ny
        d_oe_s
        g_oe_s
        very
        ever
        every

(xii)   pleas_e_
         caus_e_
         becaus_e_
         els_e_
         nois_e_

Page 6

-ay	*-oy*	*-y*
say	boy	by
day	toy	my
may	joy	why
way	an'noy	cry
pay	de'stroy	try
stay	en'joy	fry
hay	de'stroy'ing	sky
bay		cry'ing
play		
tray		
a'way		
play'ing		

-ey

they

grey

Page 7

ai	*oa*	*ea*
rain	goat	Jean
train	boat	eat
Spain	coat	seat
pain (in leg)	road (street)	sea
brain	load	meal
again	soap	meat
nail	loaf	peas
sail (ship)	oak	beans
fail	coach	peach
wait	toast	cream
paint	coast	weak
	goal	tea
		beach
		near

Page 8

oi	aw	ew
boil	saw (see)	new
coin	saw (tool)	few
soil	law	stew
oil	jaw	dew
avoid	raw	yew
hoist	awful	screw
	lawn	An'drew
	draw	drew

Page 9

-ow		-ou	
cow	tower	loud	our
now	flower	aloud	*h*our
row (noise)	shower	out	sour
how	crowd	shout	flour (cake)
town		spout	mouth
down		found	
brown		ground	
crown		sound	
owl		round	
howl			

Page 10

A. 'l' after a vowel

When a vowel is followed by *l* it often changes its sound and sometimes the *l* is not heard at all.

-all	*-alk*
all	wa*l*k
ball	ta*l*k
tall	cha*l*k
small	sta*l*k (flower)
hall	
wall	
fall	

B. 'w' before a vowel

When *w* comes before *a* the vowel sound is a short *o*.
When *w* comes before *o* the vowel sound is a short *u*.

wa-	*wo-*
was	won (race)
want	wonder
wash	wonderful
swan	worry
wander	
what	

W words with *-ar* and *-or* will be found in the Supplementary Lists, pp. 94 and 96.

Page 11

-*ight*	-*aught*	-*ought*
night	caught	bought
light	naughty	brought
tight	daughter	thought
right	taught	ought
sight	slaughter	fought
bright		nought

Notes
1. The word *high* is like *night*, *light*, etc. except that there is no *t* at the end.
2. The word *write* (with a pen) is a Page 2 word with a silent *w* on the front.
3. Mnemonic sentences for 'aught' and 'ought' words are given on p. 39.

Page 12

ow (ō)		*ew* (further words)
snow	grow	grew
row (line)	blow	blew
row (boat)	throw	threw
low	*k*now	*k*new
bow (tie)	win'dow	
bow (violin)		
sow (seed)		
slow		
show		
mow		
flow		

Page 13

(Where the vowel is long a single consonant is used; where the vowel is short the consonant needs to be doubled. *v* is an exception and is never doubled.)

-le		*-er*	
saddle	cradle	better	meter
little	title	kipper	wiper
nibble	Bible	hover	over
hobble	noble	river	diver
snuggle	bugle	ever	lever

-y		*-ed*	
tinny	tiny	batted	hated
cabby	baby	hopped	hoped
bossy	rosy	skidded	glided
jazzy	lazy	filled	filed

Note
Doubling occurs only when the next syllable starts with a vowel or (in the case of *-le*) with a vowel sound, as in the examples given above. When the next syllable begins with a consonant, as in *sadness*, doubling is unnecessary.

Page 14

		-ed	*-ing*
(i)	wait	waited	waiting
	shout	shouted	shouting
	boil	boiled	boiling
	fill	filled	filling
	stay	stayed	staying
	enjoy	enjoyed	enjoying
(ii)	hate	hated	hating
	wipe	wiped	wiping
	hope	hoped	hoping
(iii)	try (tries)	tried	trying
	cry (cries)	cried	crying
	hurry (hurries)	hurried	hurrying
	lie (lies)	lied	lying
	die (dies)	died	dying
	tie (ties)	tied	tying
(iv)	bat	batted	batting
	hop	hopped	hopping
	skid	skidded	skidding

-ly

sad – sadly   happy – happily

quick – quickly   funny – funnily

tame – tamely   gay – gaily

full – fully

Page 15

-tion

station	completion	condition	motion	solution
nation		position	promotion	resolution
relation		ignition		execution
indication		addition		revolution
operation		expedition		constitution
determination		competition		persecution
explanation		recognition		
exclamation		opposition		
temptation		composition		
discrimination				

action	correction	question
fraction	description	
subtraction	prescription	
direction	adoption	

Some extra words

Sunday	January	seven	metre
Monday	February	eight	centimetre
Tuesday	March	eleven	kilometre
Wednesday	April	twelve	
Thursday	May	thirteen	aunt
Friday	June	fourteen	uncle
Saturday	July	fifteen	cousin
	August	twenty	nephew
spring	September	thirty	niece
summer	October	forty	friend
autum*n*	November	a hundred	
winter	December	a thousand	
		a million	

month

DANGER

Dear Sir

POISON

Yours faithfully

TOILETS

POLICE

BUS STOP

Appendix II   Exercises

Exercise 1A

1. A cat sat in a bag.
2. The hen is in the box.
3. Tom sat on top.
4. Jim had a red cup.
5. The man had got a pig in the van.
6. The hut had six men in it.
7. Get a big mat and sit on it.
8. The bad dog is in the wet mud.
9. Bob is in the sun and the sun is hot.
10. Tim met a fox in the fog.

Exercise 1B

1. The fish is in the dish.
2. Shut the shed and dash up to the shop.
3. That is the thin bit of the log.
4. Bob is a big thug.
5. He had fish and chips in bed.
6. We can chop up the chest.
7. She sang a song to the men.
8. He let the tank sink in the mud.
9. A pink hat is hung on the peg.
10. I must go to the bank when I get the cash.

Exercise 1C

1. Stop on the hill and sit on the cliff top.
2. The doll will slip off the step.
3. Quick! Get the duck in the sack and stick it on that rock.
4. Has Jack lost the clock? Just check if it got left.
5. He left a mess and Dad will be cross.
6. He got a kiss from Mum and a lot of fuss.
7. Catch the milkman and fetch in the milk.
8. The witch had a black hat with a red patch on it.
9.[1] I left the badge on a ledge.
10.[2] Do not budge from the hedge till I am back.

Exercise 2A

1. Jane made a rich cake.
2. I do not like to be late, so I ride on a bike.
3. The dog came with a bone from the shop.
4. Five mice had a race to the hole.
5. We spoke to Mike and gave him a pipe to smoke.
6. The ink made a wet place on the page and the pen made a hole in it.
7. He rode home, but his bike hit a stone and he cut his nose.
8. She made such a bad joke that I did not smile.
9. His home is in quite a nice place.
10. We made a big fire on the bare stones.

Exercise 2B

1. Dick is not so spick and span as Mike.
2. The cats like to lick the plates.
3. Jack and Jane take the logs to the same place.
4. Bob left the rope on the top shelf and had to go back.
5. Mum and Dad like to take the dogs with them.

1. To be done after the pupil has learned -*ge* on Page 2.
2. Ditto.

6. It is quite time that James came home.
7. He will stack the five bikes in the shed and shut them up.
8. Slide the stuff into the boxes and make a pile.
9. Mum brushes the dust off the shelf and wipes the dishes.
10. The witches had black hats and rode on sticks.

Exercise 3A

1. If he looks, Nick can see the moon in the pond.
2. I took him to see the queen in the next street.
3. The sheep need food and a good sleep.
4. It is too good a book to drop in the mud.
5. He has seen the tools in the boot and thinks he can do the job.
6. That spoon is much too big to go in the jam dish.
7. Fetch that green brush and we will sweep up the bits of wood.
8. He had a good match but lost a boot.
9. The queen looks well in that green dress.
10. I took a sip of beer from the mug.

Exercise 3B

1. Stack the corn in that dark barn.
2. This fork is far too short for the job at the farm.
3. Jill and her sister went on under the bridge.
4. In winter it is hard to start the car.
5. Next term I will score more marks in the tests.
6. The man let him perch on the edge of the cart.
7. His sports car is in the car park next to a black van.
8. The dog will not bark if I chat to him as I go in.
9. The bench is hard to sit on for so long.
10. He had no more corn to sell, so he went back to the farm.

Exercise 4A

1. The sack fell into the pond with a big splash.
2. I need to mend her pants with a patch.

3. I for'got to thank him for the drink.
4. Bill is on hand to see to the pump if we look for him.
5. Dad lent me his sharp tools as this set is quite blunt.
6. He hopes that the band will not spend too much time in the pub.
7. He broke his arm and it is in a splint for three weeks.
8. I did not sleep a wink when I drank that strong punch.
9. His bent wire soon undid the catch.
10. I shall shunt the trucks into the shed.

Exercise 4B

1. Kate sent him a book just ten pages long.
2. Do I need to be on a bench? Can I not sleep on a soft pile of sacks?
3. I think that the twins need more lunch.
4. The dog at the farm did not bark.
5. Jane likes a rose hip drink with ice for her lunch.
6. Get them in place for the race at the fifth green tree on the left.
7. Those dogs stink. Sit them in the tub and scrub them.
8. When he sees the score he will be cross with us.
9. The cat has a gash on his left leg. Take him to the vet.
10. Mum will mend his socks in time for the trip to Leeds.

Exercise 5A[3]

1. Are we to meet the queen in the street? No, she is late.
2. Those sheep were not at the farm when I went up to see.
3. I shall have to live in Leeds in the win'ter if he gives me a job in his shop.
4. Dick was not in the park when I went to look.
5. The beer cans fell in the pond and made a big splash.
6. We were to go and fetch the milk at nine o'clock, but we were still asleep.
7. The men in the space'ship are quite safe, but have not had food for a long time.

---

3. This exercise assumes a knowledge of the words in groups (i) to (v) on Page 5.

8. Next term Jill will do Maths from a fresh text book.
9. Jim will have the same book but he likes it, so that is fine.
10. It is a good thing that Jack will not give up till he gets to the end of his sums.

Exercise 5B

1. Here are the buns in the box where I left them.
2. There are ten men in the race. Which of them will win?
3. Where did he go when I left for Man'ches'ter?
4. What plane did she catch from Manchester to Leeds?
5. Why did the boys have to go to Car'diff in March?
6. Who will tell Pat the time if she has no clock in her room?
7. The mice ran here and there under the feet of the children.
8. Where are the children? I left them here when I went to the shops.
9. Who was late for the trip to Black'pool?
10. Blackpool is a fine place to go if I am free.

Exercise 6A[4]

1. I am staying with my sister for six weeks.
2. He is playing with his toys in the bedroom.
3. She will try to pay her bills on the way to the bus stop.
4. You are in the way of the milk'man.
5. We were playing in the hay and en'joying it.
6. They say that they will try to fly the plane home.
7. Go away! You an'noy me and you are de'stroying the buds on the roses.
8. Give them back their books and keep yours safe at home.
9. Why are you crying? You can fry the fish if you wish.
10. Who is that boy trying to swim in the bay? He can do back-'stroke quite well.

4. This exercise assumes a knowledge of the words in group (vi) on Page 5.

Exercise 6B

1. What are you trying to do?
2. Where is he playing his French horn?
3. Which is your mug of milk?
4. Why did you give her our nice tray to keep?
5. Who is playing scales in the back room?
6. When did you say that she is staying in Manchester? In May?
7. The boy lives in Leeds but his sister lives in Cardiff.
8. If you must jump for joy do it in'side.
9. He was flying the plane himself.
10. If you drop the plate you will have to pay for it.

Exercise 7A[5]

1. My brother went off in the rain to catch another train.
2. Your brother has a good brain and will not fail the exam again.
3. Wait till they get to Spain and they will mend the sails at once.
4. She has a bad pain and nothing seems to help.
5. Come and sit in the sun. I have kept some food for you.
6. What have you done with the food for you that was on the shelf above the stove?
7. My son had such a lot of rain in Spain that he got on the train again.
8. The cars came to a stop, one in front of the other.
9. It is no good nailing the sail on with tacks, as they are too fine and short.
10. It is raining cats and dogs in Manchester but not in London.

Exercise 7B

1. The goat bit the coat which was hanging on the line.
2. Mother left the toast too long and it is black. Cut another slice from the loaf.
3. My brother will have to catch the other coach which comes along the coast.

---

5. This exercise assumes a knowledge of the words in group (vii) on Page 5.

4. They left the soap on the front step. What a mad thing to have done!
5. One load of hay is still at the farm. You can fetch it another day.
6. Who is that under the oak tree? I can see at once that he has a smart coat on.
7. They will get their boat on to the slip'way by the time the tide comes in.
8. He will score some goals some day.
9. The oak trees are bare in the winter, but they were green once.
10. They hung their coats on the pegs but left their boots in the yard.

Exercise 7C

1. Jean is eating a meal in one of the front rooms.
2. The others like meat but my brother eats fish.
3. Come and look at the peas and beans. They are quite big.
4. It will make it a feast if we have peaches with ice cream.
5. That tea is too weak for me. Give me another tea'bag.
6. Jean lives near the beach and can go there when she likes.
7. What sort of meal shall we have if we are going away to the sea'side?
8. They some'times sell beans and peas at the fish and chip shop.
9. Thank you; I shall eat a pink ice cream when I have had this chop.
10. Mother is shelling the peas and frying the fish for our meal.

Exercise 8[6]

1. There are a few new coins in the draw'er, and you can take one or two if you like.
2. Can I have a screw and some oil for my bike?
3. Come here and see if the stew is boiling on the stove.
4. I saw them hoist four vans up on to the ramp.
5. I gave my jaw an awful bang and I must avoid that gate in the dark.

---

6. This exercise assumes a knowledge of the words in group (viii) on Page 5.

6. That meat is still raw, so can you stew it till seven o'clock?
7. If you cut these yews with a saw I will have the law on you.
8. The dew was still on the lawn at eight o'clock this morning.
9. You will need more soil to make your lawn as flat as mine.
10. Andrew and a few other boys sat on the lawn and drew sketches.

Exercise 9A[7]

1. How now, brown cow?
2. There was such a row down in the town that I came back here.
3. The brown owl stole the crown and took it away.
4. The dogs were howling at the moon.
5. A loud shout came from the ground where my father was playing in a match.
6. They found a tea'pot on the ground where we were yes'ter'day.
7. He said that I had jam a'round my mouth and on my nose.
8. Can you give me a pound of sprouts for the other cook?
9. Out you go if you are going to run round shouting as loud as that.
10. They came near the hive but did not hear a sound from the bees.

Exercise 9B

1. What is that grey stone tower on the sky'line?
2. Try to pick the flowers soon, as they say that there will be a shower.
3. A big crowd had come together down in the town.
4. We will have to wait for hours for our bus.
5. The cream is sour, but I expect that she can make some'thing with it.
6. You need some flour for these cakes.
7. There was a big crowd round the queen when she came down the steps.
8. Keep your mouth shut and you will not get soap into it.
9. The brown owl was found on the ground.
10. Down in the town there was loud shouting.

7. This exercise assumes a knowledge of the words in group (ix) on Page 5.

Exercise 10A[8]

1. Why did you play on that wall? You were bound to fall off.
2. Two small boys and a tall one ran away with the ball.
3. It is quite a small hall and there is no room to play foot'ball.
4. Shall we talk about it as we walk to the car?
5. If I give you the chalk could you take it back to the other room?
6. A rose has sharp thorns on its stalk.
7. If you all talk at once I can'not tell what you are saying.
8. There was a crash as the box of chalk fell off the desk.
9. The name of the small man is Jack, but can you tell me who the tall one is?
10. He will tire them out by sending them all for a long walk this morning.

Exercise 10B

1. If you want to play by the farm, take care that you a'void the dog.
2. The swans were wandering round the lake when I saw them.
3. My mother is doing the washing. Do you want her?
4. Once upon a time there was a black swan which had its home far away.
5. It was wonderful when Jack won three races.
6. I wonder what he was doing in the car park?
7. That is a wonderful bunch of flowers for your mother.
8. Why worry? Something will come up in the end.
9. He is wondering if he can wander along the road and meet her?
10. She should not worry about the washing.

Exercise 11A[9]

1. There was a bright moon every night.
2. I can do very much more with my right hand than with my left.

8. This exercise assumes a knowledge of the words in group (x) on Page 5, where the 'l' changes the sound of the vowel and is silent.
9. This exercise assumes a knowledge of the words in group (xi) on Page 5.

3. It gave her a bad fright when she saw six cows on the lawn.
4. Does he get a tick if he gets it right?
5. When we get in sight of Manchester we shall be many miles from Leeds.
6. He cannot get into any of his socks as they are much too tight.
7. You look an awful sight in that dress.
8. The road goes right at the round'a'bout and it will take you to the sea.
9. Can he write with another pen so that Jill can have this one?
10. I shall not write to any'one when I am away.

Exercise 11B

1. I caught my naughty daughter and taught her not to slaughter.
2. She caught mumps when she went to stay with her sister in Kent.
3. You naughty dog! You have up'set the jar of jam on the new rug.
4. Mr and Mrs Green had two daughters.
5. However has he taught the sheep to come back to the farm when it rains?
6. I bought a football and brought it home.
7. I thought I ought to score a goal.
8. I fought hard but I still got nought.
9. What shall I do now? Shall I try to mend my bike?
10. You ought to go to Spain where the sun will make you brown.

Exercise 12[10]

1. He grew peas and beans because he did not like the ones in the shops.
2. He did not go back home until he knew that he had got the job.
3. Some time today I shall go for a row in the new boat.
4. Andrew threw the ball to Tom who caught it in his right hand.
5. Why does she want to grow such big flowers in her flat?
6. Please do not make such a noise.
7. I knew he would wonder what to do once he left London.

10. This exercise assumes a knowledge of the words in group (xii) on Page 5.

8. He was at the top of the High Street when I saw him from my window.
9. At the dress show I saw that all the dresses had small bows down the front.
10. My father is mowing the lawn and my mother is cooking the joint.

Exercise 13

1. I shall get slimmer if I keep on swimming in the river.
2. There was a bonny little rider with rosy cheeks on a tiny pony.
3. He found it quite a struggle to find a good title for his new book.
4. I saw a few new shoots on the roses today.
5. Every night for a week the wind blew and the rain came down.
6. When the bugle blew on the other side of the river he knew that he ought to get back to the camp.
7. Are you too lazy to take off that jazzy dress and slip into some slacks?
8. Above the ridge the snow was so thick that it was very hard for us to walk quickly.
9. Would you like us to give you a tow back to London?
10. He batted all day and made a big score.

Exercise 14A

1. Please come quickly as the stew has boiled dry.
2. The car glided to the end of the road but then it skidded on some oil and crashed.
3. He hopped and hopped, hoping to win the hopping race.
4. I went to the dentist who filled my tooth and filed the stopping until it was smooth.
5. He came home quite happily because he had very much enjoyed himself.
6. By tying the string tight they hoped that it would not come undone.
7. If you send the ball over the wall I shall be very an'noyed.

8. Why should I be wiping the dishes when you are just lying in bed?
9. Stop dropping lighted matches or you will cause a fire.
10. It ended funnily with the cow being found in the hall.

Exercise 14B

1. The wind blew the tiles off the roof and they broke the window in the shed.
2. It was still blowing when daylight came.
3. Throw me the plate and I will catch it without dropping it.
4. She threw it so low that I could not hang on to it.
5. Stop wandering about without looking where you are going.
6. When she left the baby in the cradle it started to babble.
7. He drew his bow across the strings and gaily played a tune.
8. She was hoping that the milkman would call daily so that she would not have to fetch the milk from the shop.
9. Daddy went over and spoke to the lady about our dinner but she had timed it for one o'clock.
10. He was lying when he told me he was out of town.

Exercise 15

1. I made an expedition to the station.
2. A revolution brought no solution to the problems of the nation.
3. Mr Jones showed much indignation over his daughter's action.
4. I was in a good position to see my relations.
5. I want an explanation. Why have you come home in this condition?
6. They did their corrections under the teacher's direction.
7. There were ten questions in the examination paper.
8. His description of Rome made me want to go there.
9. I can do subtraction sums quite quickly but I find fractions hard to understand.
10. You have displayed much determination.

Exercise 16A[11]

1. I have a suspicion that the government may decide to use coercion.
2. Cushions are out of fashion.
3. You can read the shorter version of the story on your excursion to London.
4. The mansion has no room for extension or expansion.
5. Can he afford an immersion heater if he is on a pension?
6. From the discussion at the morning session I had the impression that there was no charge for admission.
7. In his confession he said that he had been in possession of the car without the owner's permission.
8. The floats in the procession came in quick succession.
9. After the explosion everyone was feeling the tension, but there was no occasion for apprehension.
10. The mention of a new invention at once attracted his attention.

Exercise 16B[11]

1. He never failed to be generous even after he had become prosperous.
2. How courageous of you to speak when you felt so nervous!
3. Previously he had never been serious about his religious beliefs.
4. The two events were simultaneous.
5. He admitted spontaneously that his statement had been erroneous.
6. The doctor had to be cautious in case the illness was infectious.
7. I am anxious in case the noxious fumes make him unconscious if he goes into the burning house.
8. I am always suspicious of anyone who acts in an officious manner.
9. The animal was vicious and had a ferocious bark.
10. Her spelling is atrocious but her cooking is delicious.

11. Exercises 16A and 16B should not be given as part of the basic programme but are available for use with pupils who are studying Chapter 6.

Appendix III   Supplementary word-lists

e-e

these	impede	meter	tune
eve	stampede	Peter	huge
swede	centipede		tube
Swede	concede		cube
scene	intervene		mule
theme	athlete		puce
scheme	complete		rule
extreme	compete		pure
supreme	concrete		sure

u-e and ue

clue	value
cue	argue
sue	rescue
hue	avenue
Tuesday	virtue
blue	continue
glue	issue
true	residue

ea (= ĕ or ā)

head	weather	great
dead	feather	break
lead (metal)	death	steak
read (read)	breath	
instead	meant (mean)	
steady	dreamt (dream)	
ready	deaf	
already	heavy	

er sounds

ir	*ur*	*-ear*	*w + or*
girl	turn	year	work
bird	burn	earn	word
fir (tree)	fur	earnest	worm
sir	church	early	world
first	burst	earth	worse
third	nurse	learn	
thirteen	purse	search	
thirty	purple	heard	
firm	Thursday		
birthday	Saturday		

Silent letters

kn	*gn*	*wr*
knit	gnat	wrap
knot	gnaw	write
knock	gnome	wreck
knee		wring
knight		wrong
know		
knew		
knack		

ch

ch = k	*ch = sh*
school	chalet
choir	machine
chorus	chute
chord	creche
Christmas	chassis
echo	cache
anchor	
chemist	
ache	

ey and ei (= ay)

they	their	eight
grey	heir	weight
obey	vein	weigh
survey	reins	sleigh
convey	veil	neighbour
	reign	

Words in -ough

$\bar{o}$	*oo*	*ow*
though	through	plough
although		bough
dough		

off	*uff*	*-urrer*
cough	rough	thorough
trough	tough	borough
	enough	

These words should be read aloud, first of all with their sound cues (long *o*, *oo*, *off*, etc.) and afterwards without them. This should continue until they are well known, after which the spellings need not be difficult.

w + ar and au = or[1]

war	Paul
warn	haul
warm	sauce
swarm	saucer
ward	autumn
towards	cau*gh*t
	haunt
	launch
	laundry
	caution

-ie and (after 'c') ei

thief	piece	ceiling
chief	niece	conceit
grief	field	deceit
brief	wield	receive
belief	yield	perceive
relief	shield	recei*p*t
han*d*kerchief	shriek	
grieve	achieve	

---

1. The 'quar' in *quart* and *quarter* has the same sound, since *qu* is in effect equivalent to 'kw'.

Single vowel words pronounced with a long vowel or with some other sound than the regular short vowel[2]

mind	mild	old	both	most	put	truth
kind	child	bold		post	pull	Ruth
find	wild	hold			push	Hugh
rind		sold			bull	
bind		told			bush	
hind		cold				
behind						

bath	ask	last	bald
path	cask	past	scald
father	bask	cast	
rather	task	mast	
		fast	

Words with y in the middle

All the words in the following list are derived from Greek except *tyre*. Compare p. 40, footnote 4.

gym	rhythm	type
myth	cylinder	style
hym*n*	physics	tyre
		pyre

2. *wa* and *wo* words, -*all* and -*alk* words, *o* for *ŭ* words, and words in *at*, *or*, *er*, *ir*, *ur*, have not been included in these lists since they have been introduced already.

Appendix IV   Word-lists for Chapter 6

Group (i) *Words ending in -ey*[1]

honey	barley	
money	parsley	
donkey	journey	
monkey	chimney	
hockey	kidney	
jockey	abbey	
valley	turkey	Turkey
volley	jersey	Jersey
pulley		Guernsey
trolley		Anglesey

1. For discussion see pp. 44–5

Group (ii) *Words in -le and el*[2]

-le	*-el*
table	parcel
uncle	Rachel
buckle	satchel
saddle	angel
rifle	parallel
gargle	camel
ripple	panel
little	barrel
muscle	mackerel
castle	easel
bristle	tinsel
whistle	vessel
dazzle	novel
	towel
	hazel
	cruel

Exceptions: measles (*-le* instead of *-el*); and *label, rebel* (noun), *model, chapel, gospel,* and *hostel* (*-el* instead of *-le*).

Common words in -ible

terrible	sensible	(ir)responsible
horrible	(in)edible	convertible
(im)possible	(in)audible	collapsible
	(in)visible	eligible
	(il)legible	accessible
	(un)intelligible	invincible

Group (iii) *Words in -ture*[3]

nature	mixture
creature	fracture
picture	puncture
lecture	furniture
future	temperature
capture	literature

3. For discussion see p. 48.

Group (iv) *Words in -cion, -shion, -tion, -sion, and -ssion*[4]

-cion	-shion
suspicion	cushion
coercion	fashion

-tion after n and r		*-sion after n and r*	
mention	portion	pension	version
attention	proportion	tension	diversion
detention	exertion	dimension	conversion
invention	insertion	extension	aversion
prevention	assertion	mansion	submersion
intervention	desertion	expansion	immersion
	extortion	apprehension	excursion
	distortion		
	abortion		

-ssion

confession	session	mission	depression	discussion
profession	possession	admission	oppression	concussion
	accession	omission	expression	percussion
	succession	submission	impression	repercussion
	procession	permission		
	aggression	commission		
		transmission		

---

4. For discussion see p. 49.

Group (v) *Words in -age, -ace, and -ate*[5]

-age	-ace	-ate
advantage	furnace	appropriate
average	menace	certificate
bandage	palace	climate
cabbage	preface	consulate
carriage	surface	delicate
coinage	terrace	desolate
cottage		duplicate
drainage		fortunate
encourage		frigate
image		intermediate
luggage		intricate
manage		senate
marriage		subordinate
package		
passage		
postage		
savage		
shortage		
village		

5. For discussion see p. 49.

Group (vi) *Adjectives ending in -ous[6]*

a *Adjectives with a consonant or -ge- before the -ous*

famous	generous	adventurous
joyous	gorgeous	courageous
nervous	poisonous	dangerous
pompous	prosperous	tremendous

b *Adjectives ending in -ious or -eous*

bilious	harmonious	courteous
contagious	melodious	erroneous
copious	obvious	hideous
curious	religious	instantaneous
envious	serious	simultaneous
furious	various	spontaneous
glorious		

c *Adjectives with either -ci- or -ti- followed by -ous, and also -sci- and -xi- followed by -ous*

-tious	-cious	-scious	-xious
ambitious	gracious	conscious	anxious
cautious	precious	unconscious	noxious
pretentious	delicious		
licentious	suspicious		
infectious	vicious		
	ferocious		
	atrocious		
	precocious		
	officious		
	capacious		

6. For discussion see p. 50.

Group (vii) *Words in -al[7]*

Nouns in -al which can also be adjectives

		Other nouns in -al	
general	serial	trial	sandal
corporal	material	denial	rascal
principal	moral	rehearsal	dial
liberal	diagonal	betrayal	phial
cannibal	cathedral		coral
mortal	terminal		vandal
animal	aerial		cymbal
pedal			jackal
signal			medal
mineral			pedestal
funeral			interval
			hospital

Adjectives in -tial and -cial

-tial	*-cial*	
spatial	facial	beneficial
initial	racial	superficial
partial	special	social
essential	judicial	commercial
	official	crucial
	financial	
	provincial	

7. For discussion see pp. 50–2.

Group (viii) *Common words in -ent and -ant*[8]

-ent		-ant	
Nouns	*Adjectives*	*Nouns*	*Adjectives*
accident	absent	assailant	abundant
client	apparent*	assistant	brilliant
continent	confident	attendant	defiant
current (water or electricity)	consistent*	consultant	distant
gradient	convenient	contestant	dominant
opponent	different	currant (fruit)	fragrant
Orient	eloquent	descendant	gallant*
parent	evident	elephant	indignant*
resident	excellent	giant	instant
serpent	frequent*	infant	luxuriant
student	impudent	informant	observant
talent	independent	inhabitant	pleasant
	insolent	merchant	radiant
	obedient	participant	relevant
	permanent	peasant	vigilant
	prominent	pheasant	
	silent	tenant	
	violent	truant	

8. For discussion see p. 53.
Note. All adjectives have corresponding nouns ending in *-ance* and *-ence* except those marked*.

Readers, workbooks, and materials

Note: We have made no attempt to make the following lists comprehensive but have limited ourselves to items which we ourselves have found helpful and which we believe can be used to advantage by parents and teachers.

Readers

Choice of the correct level of reader (reading book) is particularly important in the case of a dyslexic child. If you are starting at the very beginning we recommend that strictly phonic readers should be used (i.e. those which contain words where there is a simple match between their sound and their component letters) such as the following:

Primary Phonics and *More Primary Phonics*, by Barbara Makar. Cambridge, Mass., Educators' Publishing Service,[1] 1969 seq. (Each of these two sets comprises 10 books; we have found Sets 1 and 2 particularly helpful in the early stages.)

One Way with Words, by Anne-Marie Gillam. Bath, Better Books,[2] 1980. (21 books)

Tempo Books, by Paul Groves and Leslie Stratta. London, Longman, 1966 seq. (10 books; 8–9½ year reading level, 11–16 year interest level.)

Look Out Gang, by M. B. Chaplin. Glasgow, Robert Gibson & Sons, 1968. (6 books, of which Book One and Book Two are particularly helpful in the early stages.)

1. Full address: 75 Moulton St, Cambridge, Mass., 02138, USA.
2. Full address: 15A Chelsea Road, Lower Weston, Bath. Better Books is also the UK agent for Educators' Publishing Service.

Royal Road series, by J. C. Daniels and H. Diack. London, Chatto & Windus, 1957 seq.

Bangers and Mash, by Paul Groves. London, Longman, 1975 seq.

Beginner Books, by Dr Seuss and others. Glasgow, Collins, 1958 seq.

Workbooks

Sure-Fire Phonics, by Ann Williams and Jim Rogerson. Exeter, Wheaton, 1980. (6 books, suitable for the early stages.)[3]

Space to Spell, by Frula Shear, Judith Raines, and Diana Targett. Bath, Better Books, 1975.

Sounds Travel Too, by Sonia Machanick. London, Heinemann, 1969. (4 books)

Read, Write, and Spell, by Julia Leech and Gillian Nettle. London, Heinemann, 1978. (4 books)

Logical Spelling, by B. V. Allan. Glasgow and London, Collins,[3] 1977.

Gay Way Books, by E. R. Boyce. London, Macmillan, 1954 seq. (4 books)

Super Spelling Books, by Charles Cuff with David Mackay. Harlow, Longman, 1981. (6 books)

Solving Language Difficulties, by A. Steere, C. Z. Peck, and L. Kahn. Cambridge, Mass., Educators' Publishing Service, 1979. (Mostly concerned with prefixes, suffixes and syllable work.)[3]

Learn to Spell, by S. D. Wright. Welwyn Garden City, James Nisbet, 1975.

Exercise your Spelling, by Elizabeth Wood. London, Arnold, 1982. (3 books)

Materials

Blank playing cards are available from Better Books (see footnote p. 107 for address).

Nylon pen grips are available from Taskmaster Ltd, Leicester.

The *Edith Norrie Letter Case* is available from the Helen Arkell

---

3. These workbooks are re-usable.

Dyslexia Centre, 14 Crondace Road, London SW6. Enquiries should also be made at this address about the *Tutorpack* teaching machine and the exercises for it.

The *Stott Programmed Reading Kit* is available from Holmes and McDougall Ltd, Edinburgh.

Phonetic Word Drill Cards, *Word Blends*, *Word Prefixes*, and *Word Suffixes*, published by Kenworthy, Buffalo, New York, are available from Better Books (see footnote p. 107 for address).

Coloured cards, *felt pens*, and *biros with eraser tops* can be bought at most stationers.

Suggestions for further reading

Books on teaching

M. Hooton (1976) *The First Reading and Writing Book*, London, Heinemann.

B. Hornsby and F. Shear (1977) *Alpha to Omega*, London, Heinemann.

J. Pollock (1978) *Signposts to Spelling*, London, Helen Arkell Dyslexia Centre.

Background reading

A. Ansara (ed.), *Current Issues in Dyslexia, Bulletin of the Orton Society*, xxix, 1979.

M. Critchley (1970) *The Dyslexic Child*, London, Heinemann.

M. and E. A. Critchley (1978) *Dyslexia Defined*, London, Heinemann.

A. W. Franklin and S. Naidoo (eds) (1970) *Assessment and Teaching of Dyslexic Children*, London, The Invalid Children's Aid Association.

A. Gillingham and B. E. Stillman (1969) *Remedial Training for Children with Specific Disability in Reading, Spelling and Penmanship*, Cambridge, Mass., Educators' Publishing Co.

H. K. Goldberg and G. B. Schiffman (1972) *Dyslexia. Problems of Reading Disabilities*, New York, Grune and Stratton Inc.

J. Jansky and K. de Hirsch (1973) *Preventing Reading Failure*, New York, Harper and Row.

T. R. Miles (1978) *Understanding Dyslexia*, London, Hodder & Stoughton.

T. R. Miles (1983) *Dyslexia: The Pattern of Difficulties*, St Albans, Granada Publishing Co.

S. Naidoo (1972) *Specific Dyslexia*, London, Pitman.

M. Newton, M. E. Thomson, and I. J. Richards (1979) *Readings in Dyslexia*, Wisbech, Bemrose, UK Ltd.

G. Th. Pavlidis and T. R. Miles (eds) (1981) *Dyslexia Research and Its Applications to Education*, Chichester, John Wiley & Sons.

M. B. Rawson (1978) *Developmental Language Disability: Adult Accomplishments of Dyslexic Boys*, Cambridge, Mass., Educators' Publishing Service.

B. H. Slingerland (1971) *A Multisensory Approach to Language Arts for Specific Language Disabled Children*, Cambridge, Mass., Educators' Publishing Service.

Those interested may like to subscribe to the *Dyslexia Review*, obtainable from the Dyslexia Institute, 133 Gresham Road, Staines, Middlesex. Those wishing to receive the *Annals of Dyslexia*, formerly the *Bulletin of the Orton Society*, should write to The Orton Society, 8415 Bellona Lane, Towson, Maryland 21204, USA. Parents may also like to read the leaflet, *Suggestions for Helping the Dyslexic Child in the Home*, by Marion Welchman, which is obtainable from Better Books, 15A Chelsea Road, Lower Weston, Bath (tel. 0225-28010).

Where to go for help

Australia	SPELD, PO Box 94, Mosman 2088, New South Wales
Denmark	Ordblindeinstituttet, Calissensvej 34, Hellerup
New Zealand	SPELD, PO Box 13391, Christchurch
Norway	Specialskolen for Thalehemmed, Bredtvet, Oslo 9
UK	(i) The British Dyslexia Association, Church Lane, Peppard, Oxfordshire RG9 5JN
	(This is the headquarters from whom particulars of the nearest local Association can be obtained.)
	(ii) The Dyslexia Institute, 133 Gresham Road, Staines, Middlesex TW18 2AJ
	(iii) The Helen Arkell Centre, 14 Crondace Road, London SW6
USA	The Orton Dyslexia Society, 8415 Bellona Lane, Towson, Maryland 21204
	(This is the headquarters from whom particulars of the nearest local branch of the Society can be obtained.)

Index